TIMELY WISDOM

50 VALUABLE INSIGHTS INTO LIFE

BY ROBERT W. LAWRENZ

Other books by Robert William Lawrenz

I Remember... Thoughts on a Well-Lived Life
How To... Build a Meaningful Career
Devotional Stories: Good News of Great Joy

Timely Wisdom
By Robert William Lawrenz
robertwlawrenz@gmail.com

Associate Editor: Roger Luoma
Editor: Dawn Sjolund
Technical: Paul Sjolund
Cover Design by: Kiersten Sjolund

Printed in the United States of America

ISBN: 9781500969790

DEDICATION

To the coming generation, I dedicate this book:

Marie, Tim and Jonas Magnuson, Shari Sjolund, Kiersten Sjolund, Brynn Lawrenz, and Robert Ken Lawrenz

God's blessings are not an end in themselves but an encouragement to take the next step in faith.

FIRST THOUGHTS

In 2002 we moved to Eden Prairie, Minnesota from Rockford, Illinois. At that time in my life I was looking for new challenges. I began writing as a new career. Writing requires two things, having something to say and being able to say it clearly. I had lots of things I want to say but my writing skills were marginal so I had to reinvent myself. Over the years I have improved my writing skills.

For about the first five years I was content to write Insights into life. At the urging of my son who thought I had a very eventful life, I began writing my first book, an autobiography called *I Remember.*

About the same time I began writing for Wooddale Church and authored about 50 articles, which I later published in my third book *Good News of Great Joy.*

After my first book I wrote a second book on *How to Build a Meaningful Career.* This responds to the many people I have encounted at the crossroads of life that were unable to sort things out and establish a new direction.

My fourth book *Timely Wisdom* is a selection of 50 of the more than 100 Insights I have written. Insight means seeing clearly into the fundamental nature of reality. True wisdom is not thinking smart. There are many smart people who come up with the wrong conclusions. True wisdom comes from having knowledge, understanding, and being able to apply it. It requires perspective and a good moral compass.

Over the and years a number of people have told me I have the gift of wisdom. I will let you be the judge.

CONTENTS

PERSONAL INSIGHTS

CULTURAL INSIGHTS

SPIRITUAL INSIGHTS

PERSONAL INSIGHTS

TOPIC #1
Why I am a Happy Camper

I am a happy guy. I began to wonder why.

My research led to Martin Seligman's *Positive Psychology*, which gave me the insight as to why I am basically a happy person. His approach was to understand what made people healthy and well adjusted rather than dealing with sickness and psychological disorders.

Happiness is a state of well-being. It is a feeling than rather an emotion, and is therefore a result of your decisions about attitude towards life. Years ago, I decided to be optimistic and always look for the up-side possibilities first.

The basis of authentic happiness is having a purpose-driven life *and* the practice of virtue.

Choosing a Purpose-Driven Life

For the purpose-driven life there are number of choices: Power, fame and fortune have been classic, but for most of us it is being a good husband/father or a good wife/mother or being a good employee. For me it has been 1) loving God and serving him, 2) being an exemplary husband/father/grandfather/provider and 3) being successful at my career/business.

The challenge of life is to balance or to focus on your drives within the limitations of your time and energy. I chose to balance, which means compromise, but I did increase my efficiency by integrating ministry into my business. An understanding and supportive wife was greatly enabling. My kingdom work was primarily encouraging, counseling, caring for and enabling others, which is multiplication strategy. Some examples of kingdom building: Twenty-five years ago I organized and led a team of people to build an apartment in Dottie Haun's basement to provide free living accommodations for missionaries and others who needed short-term housing. It is still in use today. Thirty years ago I encouraged a new Laotian convert to Christianity to enter the ministry. He is currently the pastor of three churches. Ten years ago I stood by a pastor, who was not equipped for the pastoral ministry, but is now effectively serving in an evangelism ministry partly due to my moral support. Ten years ago Lura and I, through a small group, influenced a couple to have a personal relationship with Christ, which saved their marriage. They have become active witnesses and active in their church. Recently we saw a young married, pregnant Chinese woman find God and Christ through caring friendship. This multiplication makes life purposeful!

Being Virtuous

Virtue is goodness or godliness. All virtue is endowed in the human soul at the time of the creation and reflects the character of God. It is still part of the human spirit although corrupted by our sinful nature. Virtue, coupled with purpose, is essential for authentic happiness. Adolf Hitler and Joseph Stalin were power driven but not virtuous and therefore unhappy men.

There are two types of virtue. Virtue of the Heart: love, compassion, gifting, honor, optimism; and Virtue of the Mind: self- discipline, determination, orderliness, duty. The challenge for happiness is to capitalize on using the virtues that come naturally. Of all the virtues, gifting is the most essential one for happiness. It reflects God himself who gave his precious Son. There is something special about giving ourselves away in the form of volunteering time, expertise or money that make us happy. When I founded Focus Financial Advisors I adopted a policy of giving 10% of my time to clients who could not afford

3

my services. I invested thousands of hours helping widows, missionaries, pastors and others who had limited income.

One experience was with a divorced woman who had been emotionally destroyed by a controlling husband, was alienated from her children, had no place to live, was $100,000 in debt, had child support to pay and no employment for income. I worked with her for years and now she has a fine Christian husband, her own home, restored relationships with her children, a positive net worth, an attractive salary and is active in her church. She has found true happiness.

Christians have a special access to happiness. When they invite Christ into their heart and life, the Holy Spirit enters their soul and gives "spiritual gifts." These gifts may complement natural birth gifts or be different. Leith Anderson, a gifted pastor and teacher, describes himself as naturally introverted but God gave him the spiritual gift of leadership. He has both purpose and virtue which give him energy and a happy spirit for contributing to the kingdom of God. As Frederick Buechner says, "God's call on your life is where your greatest gladness meets the world's greatest need."

Now I know why I am a HAPPY guy!

TOPIC #2
How the Mind Bends and Works

The mind is a bewilderment. It may be the epitome of God's greatest creation.

The central nervous system is the ultimate in sophistication consisting of two hemispheres, five regions, four lobes, three pathways for moving impulses, 210 nuclei (groups of similar cells that serve a function) and billions of axon and dendrite cells. The mind can imagine by projection and tell the difference between reality and fantasy. It has self awareness. It can be controlled to rest, clear or empty itself. It can be rational or illogical. It can be convinced of anything, as with anorexia. It can be cognitive or incoherent. It is amazingly plastic and able to heal and change itself.

How does the mind work? It works through the brain. The brain is one of the largest organs in the body, weighing more than 3 pounds. While it only constitutes about 2% of a body's weight, it receives 20% of the blood supply and consumes 20% to 25% of energy used by the body.

Dr. Mary Ezzo says that when a child is born, he will have about the same number of brain cells that he will have as an adult. What changes dramatically during brain development is the way those cells connect and wire-up. We have an estimated 100 billion neurons or nerve cells which look like a tree with a long trunk called an axon (axons send messages out of the nerve cell) and the branches are called dendrites (dendrites receive incoming messages). Nerve cells never actually touch. Instead, they send and receive all information in the form of 60 different chemicals called neurotransmitters that move through an estimated 500 trillion synapse or gaps between dendrites and axons. The most common of these chemicals have names like

GABA, glutamate, dopamine, serotonin and norepinephrine. It is the balance of these chemicals that drives behavior. High norepinephrine usually manifests itself as impulsivity. It is our fight-or-flight chemical. Low serotonin rears its head as depression. Drugs have been invented to off-set chemical imbalances.

God's incredible design is that each chemical has a distinct shape that permits it to bind only to a perfectly matched receptor in the body. There is a perfect lock-and-key order to the interplay of chemicals.

During development the brain cells of fetus brain cells are multiplying at the rate of 250,000 per minute. Between the ages of birth and 10, the child's brain undergoes vast increases in the number of dendrites on each brain cell (neuron). The neurons of the growing child make twice as many connections as the child will ever need. The dramatic learning in the child's brain is not a growth of new brain cells. Rather, it is the tremendous proliferation of the dendrites on each cell and therefore the enormous potential that occurs through the connections it can make. It is imperative that a child has as much interpersonal contact and stimulation as possible. At age 2 the child's brain is mapping out the sound and meaning of about 10 new words a day. Between ages 10 through 20, the brain starts to prune the connections that have not been used. All of this excess capacity explains how children can acquire language and memorize facts faster than adults. After age twenty, the emphasis should be on understanding how things work and on wisdom, which is applying knowledge and understanding.

While we know a great deal about the physiology of the brain, we do not fully understand how the frontal cortex, which serves as the place for our working memory, can decide what to send to the hippocampus, for long-term memory, or how it can instantly recall specific information about an event, that occurred 40 years ago, from the hippocampus and the associated emotion from the amygdale. While memories are not actually stored in the hippocampus, they reside encoded in the brain's corrugated six layers called the neocortex. Each layer operates uniquely in a hierarchical structure with millions of columns moving impulses up and down forming invariant patterns and sequences. First we learn individual letters (A,B,C), then patterns (CAT not C-A-T) then sequences (FAT CAT). When invariant patterns or sequences of information are sent down the layers, if it is not recognized, it is sent back up to the hippocampus where it is determined where it should be discarded or returned to the cortex. Thus, without a hippocampus we could not learn anything new but could remember previously learned things. Memory can be a curse if it remembers (or forgets) too much or too little. It is a conundrum how the brain can simultaneously perform multiple tasks, such as playing the piano and singing.

The frontal cortex is the area in your brain that conducts judgment and that enables you to foresee the implications of your decisions. It is the place where you make the hard decisions, like how to save for retirement rather than spend. It is this part of the brain that makes us truly different from animals.

About one third of the brain is devoted to our visual capacity which explains why we learn so much more efficiently when we can see or imagine something. We do not see with our eyes. The eyes only project form, motion and color through the optic never so seeing is a construct within the visual cortex. What we do not understand is how the brain can record in the visual cortex so much visual input and temporarily store it but later discard it. If you are a passenger in a car that travels for an entire day, you are exhausted even though you did nothing but sit. What has happened is your brain has had to absorb tens of thousands of visual inputs and this tires you out.

While we understand how the brain works, we do not understand how it learns and self-governs. The fundamental tools of thought are: experience, memory, association, reason, invention, experimentation, intuition and pattern discernment, and recognition. Sleep seems to have something to do with it, because our controlling frontal cortex rests while the reminder of the brain re-boots during the night which explains why things are so much clearer the next morning and why dreams are so uninhibited.

States of Mind

In the case of one who believes in God, the mind can be controlled by the Holy Spirit. If the mind is cognizant and healthy, it can be under the control of the Holy Spirit and produce a mind state of love, joy and peace, and prompt the mind with godly thoughts.

The mind can also be controlled by spirits. The spirits produce a mind state of fear, anger and confusion and fill the mind with depression, rage or irrational violence, e.g., O.J. Simpson, Scott Peterson and Cho Seung-Hui (Ismael Ax) who are psychopaths who kill without feeling. These conditions frequently manifest themselves in physical symptoms, extreme behavior or psychological abnormalities, such as hearing voices.

Sad eyes or facial expression can be good indicators of spirit possession. We saw this with Laotians whose faces went from sad to happy when they accepted Christ as savior. A happy-faced Laotian lady came up to me and started talking to me like I knew her, but I did not recognize her. It was because the last time we had met she had a deadpan face. She had found Jesus and he changed her countenance. We also saw this with a friend, who had serious health problems and depression over a number of years, until a spirit was exorcized. Her face and eyes changed, and she was freed from her physical problems.

8

The brain can be self-controlled and operational on its own cognizance. Even the healthy mind uses mental mechanisms like rationalization, compensation, substitution, subordination, etc., to deal with reality. The mind can be manipulated, consciously or unconsciously (such as labyrinths, where you use a prescribed path to reconnect with your inner wisdom) or anorexia, where a person sees himself as fat even though he may be very thin.

Keep your mind healthy by keeping it active with good thoughts, imagination and inputs and eat lots of blueberries. God created for you the most wonderful mind/brain capability he could think of! Be a good steward of your mind. Use it wisely and up to its full potential.

TOPIC #3
Is Your Life Meaningful and Significant?

In order to have a meaningful and significant life you need to understand what it is and how to do it. The following scenarios will assist you in this process. See how many differences you can identify between Bert, the pragmatist, and Wally, the realist.

* * *

Hi, it is nice to meet you Bert. What do you do for a living?
"Oh I am just a janitor at the Wilson school."

What kind of responsibilities do you have?
"Well, I clean and restock the bathrooms three times a week. You know how messy kids are and the toilets frequently get plugged-up. I replace burned-out light bulbs on a rotation schedule. I mop the floors and pick up trash. It is my responsibility to see that an annual checkup of all the air conditioners is done by a sub-contractor."

That sounds like a rewarding job.
"Yes, every Friday when I get paid."

What plans do you have for your future?
"I plan on keeping my present job until I retire. You know I love to play golf and watch TV."

* * *

Hi, it is nice to meet you Wally. What do you do for a living?
"Oh I am a janitor at the Wilson school."

What kind of responsibilities do you have?

10

"Well, I sanitize the bathrooms twice a day. Germs spread pretty rapidly in bathrooms, you know, so protecting the kids' health is important. I replace burned-out light bulbs in the stairwells because people are more likely to stumble if they can't see well. Our school has a very good safety record. I mop the floors and pick up trash to keep our good image up to standard. It is my responsibility to do the annual checkup of all the air conditioners. I had training so we do not have to call in a costly sub-contractor. It is part our school's cost-control program."

That sounds like a rewarding job.
"Yes, I have a good relationship with the teaching staff, the principal and the kids. We have a good team so I look forward to going to work most days."

What plans do you have for your future?
"My wife and I having been saving up so I can retire early. We are planning on going to Mozambique for an extended mission trip. I understand there is a need to train men in mechanics and my wife is a nurse and gifted teacher."

MEANINGFUL

Having a meaningful life requires a positive attitude, insight and a passion for excellence. It is building relationships. It is having a worldview that sees the world in need. It is enjoying life while serving others. Meaning flows from the heart.

Doing something can be rewarding and can provide some degree of satisfaction, but for something to be meaningful it has to accomplish something beneficial. If you cut down a tree in the forest you have done something. If you cut the tree up into firewood and give to an elderly person so he can heat his home, you are doing something that can become a meaningful act.

SIGNIFICANT

Significance is having an impact on the world. It is about multiplying yourself or expanding something. It is using imagination. It is seizing opportunities. It requires thinking and planning. It is enjoying seeing success. Significance flows from the mind. Measurement is important in determining the significance of a program. What gets measured gets done.

While meaning is qualitative, significance is quantitative. Teaching one man to be a mechanic is significant, however it is more significant to teach ten and even more significant to teach one hundred. Bill Bright, the founder of Campus Crusade for Christ, led people to Christ one at a time using the *Four Spiritual Laws* pamphlet. But when he created the *Jesus* film millions found Christ.

While you do not have to be Christian to have a life of meaning and significance, it is the abundant life Jesus promised to those who are Believers. John 10:10 says, "...I have come that they may have life, and have it to the full." Enjoy a life that is both meaningful and significant.

TOPIC #4
What is Good Leadership?

Leadership has been a "hot topic" for more than 50 years. There seem to be as many theories on the subject as there are authorities on it. I believe the lack of consensus is due to the confusion between the concepts of management and leadership.

Management is setting goals – outcomes, strategy--how things will be done, and tactics – what needs to be done. Management is accomplished through control, directing, communication, teaching, assigning authority and responsibility, and modeling. It is not time or circumstance driven. Management authority can be granted or assumed.

Leadership is having a vision and being able to cast it. It is not enough to just have a vision. You must be able to get your followers to understand what you want accomplished. They must adopt your vision as their own. History seems to show that leadership is earned and seems to be time-and-circumstance driven. Being the right person, at the right time and in the right place seems to be necessary for leaders to be successful. That is why it is imperative that you follow God's leading. Leadership is giving people freedom to act, not controlling them. It is letting things flow.

Management may be necessary for a time before leadership takes place. Jesus' ministry followed this sequence pattern. He spent the first three years managing by teaching, directing and modeling. He sent his disciples out two-by-two with the authority to heal and cast out spirits, but this was limited by their faith. When they were well trained they were ready for the transition to leadership. After Jesus' death and resurrection, He appeared to them and gave them a vision that lasted them through great difficulties and for the rest of their lives. They

13

were no longer directed as to what to do. They knew what to do. They were set free to minister as the Spirit led and were successful at their vision of spreading the gospel of salvation through the death and resurrection of Jesus to the world.

There is a question as to whether you should lead and manage by being upfront or by managing from behind. Management requires an upfront positioning. You need to constantly make the decisions and give direction. Poor management is having a wrong strategy, giving poor direction or having a lack of focus, which causes confusion. Things just will not flow. This produces high turnover, marginal performance and low morale.

Leadership can be done upfront or from the back. Upfront leadership is like a General leading a cavalry charge with his drawn saber pointing toward the objective. It requires teaching and modeling. Leading from behind is less stressful but more risky. The leader must be sure he has instilled the vision and has cast it in such a way that people understand it and adopt it as their own. If they do not share the vision, you will be perceived as a weak leader. What matters is giving people freedom to carry out the vision once it is theirs.

Leading from behind is best understood by looking at the horses pulling a Wells Fargo stagecoach. Once the horses have a vision for the grain and rich green pastures that await them at journey's end, their passion for the rewards will take over. The leader's job becomes encouraging and occasionally giving direction by a slight tug on the reins. Every driver must know his team well. Some of the horses will be sprinters, which carry the load during the first part of the trip, and others will have endurance to carry the load toward the end of the journey. The driver's task is to develop the team effort in such a way that each horse has the freedom to contribute to the total effort.

In the 1980's thousands of Laotian refugees came to the United States. They were ardent Buddhists. For three years I taught the Scriptures to about 100 of them without results. Then one of the Laotian leaders, whose wife had severe physical and emotional problems, was cared for by loving Christian women. The leader realized that these women loved his wife more than he did. It was a defining moment, and he gave his life to Christ. Then hundreds of Laotians came to know Christ as their Savior. Some went for theological training and became pastors, church leaders, and teachers. They founded a church and built a million-dollar worship center. Today they are devoted Christians committed to winning others to Christ. Once they had the vision and it was theirs, things began to flow and little direction was needed.

Which is better? It depends where your strength is, in managing or in leading. Managing always works but the rewards of leadership are greater. Management and leadership can be implemented either in sequence or concurrently. If they are done by two different people, doing them concurrently requires coordination and cooperation.

Management is about control. Leadership is about giving people the freedom to realize the vision.

TOPIC #5
Preparing to be a Leader

We are all leaders; it is just a matter of the time or circumstances. We become leaders of our children, grandchildren, spouses, employees, or in our neighborhoods, churches etc. But how do we become effective leaders? How does GOD PREPARE US FOR LEADERSHIP?

1) God provides us with the necessary training we need for the challenge.
2) He provides us with the necessary experiences we need to make us ready.
3) During the challenge, He provides us with those who will help, advise and/or give us encouragement.
4) God will enable us even though we may feel inadequate to meet the challenge.
5) He will support us even when we make mistakes.
6) He will tell us when our mission is completed.

We can see this preparation process in the life of Moses.

He was trained by his birthmother about the history of his ethnic origins and trained in the courts of Pharaoh where he received a PhD in speech and engineering. His experience during his forty years in the desert taught him "wilderness survival skills" and how to lead as a shepherd of sheep. These experiences on how to find water in the desert and on how to lead sheep (even though some do not follow or go astray or are belligerent) would give him the skill sets that he would apply later in life. He received the encouragement he needed from his mother and from his father-in-law Jethro who advised him on how to organize the judicial system with District Courts and a Supreme Court. He had Aaron as his Executive Vice President in charge of operations.

16

Moses was willing, "Here I am Lord," but lacked the self-confidence to follow God's instructions. God understood him and gave him the faith to proceed with the power to perform miracles and gave him Aaron to compensate for his feelings of insecurity.

God gave Moses the vision of the Promised Land; Moses in turn communicated it to the people. Most caught the vision but those who did not wanted to return to the slavery of Egypt, if you can imagine that! It is vision that gives us the energy to achieve the goal. Without vision we settle for the status quo or revert back to mediocrity.

Moses had an anger problem that caused him to make three major mistakes. He killed an Egyptian slave driver in anger. In anger over the people's blatant sin he broke the tablets where God had just inscribed the Ten Commandments. In anger he struck the rock for water rather than speaking to it as God had instructed. In each case God understood and responded. God used the killing of the Egyptian as a "defining monument" in Moses' life to change the course of human history. God solved the problem of the broken tablets by replacing them. God responded to the use of the rod on the rock by giving him water anyway. But God did use the incident to tell Moses that his ministry would end when they reached the border of the Promised Land. It would be time for new fresh leadership, without the interference of Moses, but with his legacy.

Moses must have had mixed emotions as he stood at Mount Nebo looking over the Promised Land, which he would never enter. He had succeeded in his leadership challenge to lead the people to the goal; but not without setbacks and problems. If we are wise vision-leaders, God will reward us with personal satisfaction, if we do not dwell on the collateral damage.

TOPIC #6
Being an Effective Leader

Leadership is casting a vision. Vision is imagining an outcome. Imagination is unique to the human mind. It is seeing in the "mind's eye" what cannot be seen with the real physical eye. It is dreaming. It is wondering, cogitating or inkling about something until you understand it. It is what Malcolm Gladwell in his book *Blink* describes as a "thin slice" where your mind uses intuition to fill in the whole with just a bit of information.

The human mind is unique in that it can not only imagine, it can tell the difference between fact and fantasy. When you wake up in the morning your dream seems so real, but you know it was fantasy. People who cannot distinguish between fact and fantasy are called delusional.

Vision leadership is demonstrated in the Bible. Abraham led his family on a pilgrimage to a land he could only imagine. Moses led his people to a promised land. Joseph had a dream about his leadership and how he could help the people survive a famine.

How do we develop imagination? We develop it with the arts, not science. The Massachusetts Institute of Technology (MIT) only accepts students who have demonstrated natural leadership because they know that a technical education will not develop leaders. Science is fact finding and analysis which are "doer" skills not leadership skills. Philosophy forces our mind to think conceptually. Music and art produces emotions that are expressed as feelings which give us empathy and good listening skills. Pottery and architecture are the physical shape and form of an idea or concept. History requires us to imagine how things happened before our time. Writing or reading novels and poetry are imagery expressed in words. Listening to a radio program, unlike TV, requires imagination. Psychology enables us to see how the human psyche works. Think about all of the frustrated scientists whose patents are issued for products that are never sold because no one has the insight to see how it can be used.

Leadership and management are different skills and are rarely native to the same person. Two of my life experiences will demonstrate my point.

Tom McCullough was a talented Vice President of Manufacturing at National Lock Company. Tom died unexpectedly at age 42. The President and I decided that we would take our time in finding a good engineering-type to replace Tom. Within two weeks the manufacturing operation was falling apart. Tom was a manager who made all the decisions and had a staff who could carry out his orders. Tom was an effective manager but not a leader. Organizations can run well with managers in charge but do not run well when they are not present to make decisions. Managers do not empower people like leaders.

At that time, as the Controller of the company, I became the Vice President of Manufacturing because of my leadership skills. I began to think and plan on a thirteen-week horizon, not on the week-by-week management style of Tom. I went to a seminar in California to gain an understanding of electroplating so I could give direction to something I knew nothing about. I trained the staff to be decision-makers instead of order-takers. I successfully led the manufacturing function for eight years without any manufacturing background.

My first job was as a Budget Analyst with Bell & Howell Company in Chicago. I was at the doer level and saw the company from the bottom up. Chuck Percy was the first man under age thirty to be the President of a Fortune 500 Company. Chuck was a strong leader who gave books to his staff to stimulate their thinking skills. Chuck had an iron-handed

Executive Vice President, Bill Roberts, who managed the company. Chuck did not spend much of his time at the office and always had a clean desk.

Then the Board of Directors hired Peter G. Peterson, an advertising executive from McCann Erickson Agency, to be President of the company's largest operating division. It was a disaster! However, after two years he was promoted to corporate Chief Executive Officer and Percy left to become a U.S. Senator. As corporate CEO Peterson did an outstanding job of leading and went on to be The Secretary of Commerce and then to be the CEO of Lehman Brothers, one of the world's largest investment banking firms. He was the Chairman of the Council on Foreign Relations and the author of a number of books. He was one of the founders of the Blackstone Group, a private-equity, asset management and financial advisory firm that made him a billionaire.

At the time it was difficult to understand how the Board of Directors could promote such a failure. However the Board saw him as an outstanding leader and his job managing an operating division was a training ground to prepare him for the top job.

There are doers, managers and leaders. Organizations with the right people at all three levels are the ones that truly thrive over time.

TOPIC #7
Learning – An Important Discipline

What is learning?
Learning is the lifelong disciplined process of acquiring Knowledge – facts, gaining Understanding – how things fit together or work and then formulizing Wisdom – seeing complex or subtle things in simplistic terms. This process requires a teachable spirit. A spelling bee is an example of the learning process. The contestant is tested on his Knowledge – spelling the word correctly. But to help him know the right word to spell he is given its definition to improve his Understanding and then it is used in a sentence to help him see its application – Wisdom.

All knowledge is acquired through one or more of our five senses and through intuition or imagination (Polanyi 1891-1976 *Tacit Knowing: Truthful Knowing*). Dining with someone is one of the few activities that involve all five of our senses. That may be the reason that we enjoy eating so much! When the hippocampus part of your brain receives input, much of the chatter and clutter is discarded, but the facts and events are stored in the consciousness of our long-term memory. This declarative memory is the "know that" function that makes a good speller.

Understanding is the perceiving and comprehending the nature and significance of knowledge. It is applying logic or reason to the eight fundamentals of thought: experience, memory, association, pattern discernment and recognition, reason, invention, experimentation and intuition. It is analysis or critical thinking to imagine outcomes. It is creative thinking, sometimes outside the box. It is the intelligent assembly of facts. It is the procedural memory of the "know how" and takes place in the basal ganglia where skills are learned and the cerebellum where associative learning takes place. Efficacy in

21

this area makes a good speller into champion speller (*Baker Encyclopedia of Psychology and Counseling*, Page 737).

Wisdom is discernment; the power to see what is not evident to the average mind and to distinguish and select what is true. To acquire knowledge one must study but to acquire wisdom, one must observe. Wisdom is applying understanding into truth. Wisdom can be as simple as common sense or require a great deal of time for insightful introspection and contemplation. Wisdom can be used for evil, cunning, or for good, benevolence. Mistakes and misconceptions are the learning process but something is not learned until it changes behavior for good. Even Solomon with all his wisdom hadn't learned everything. Wisdom comes to those who ask God for it.

There was a man who went to Africa to farm. Over time he developed 21 improvements in his farming methods which he taught to the Africans. Eventually he left Africa leaving behind all the successful methods he had perfected and taught. Five years later an audit was conducted that revealed that none of his improvements were still in use. Why did he fail? He had taught the knowledge of farming, maybe some understanding, but no wisdom. Learning has not taken place until knowledge, understanding how things work, and the wisdom to apply them are all present.

Learning comes from your personal experience or from others. Learning others' experience is called education. Formal education begins at age 6 and by age 18 based on our God-given talents, interests and capabilities we should have a life mission mapped out as to what we want to accomplish in life. Now you should concentrate 50% of your education on your specialty and 50% on a broad base of other subjects. This will give you the expertise and credentials you need for employment and still be a well-balanced person. However there are no jobs for spelling champions!

TOPIC #8
Personal Growth = Life Changes

One of our core values is growth. Personal growth covers every aspect of our lives. It is becoming a balanced holistic person with focus in strategic areas. Spiritual growth is the centerpiece of growth.

Growth by definition is change; change is movement. What then do we change? Over time we acquire a certain worldview, core values, patterns of thinking, formulas for decision-making and instinctive behavioral reflexes. These bring order to our life. However, once established these reflexes can go beyond habits to deeply ingrained behaviors and on to enslaving addictions. For substantive change to occur we need a biblical worldview, renewed thinking, the modeling of Christ and the insight and power of the Holy Spirit. There are real limits on what we can change with good intentions, resolve or discipline. Perfecting our worldview, core values and mind-set is the prerequisite for significant movement.

Personal growth is a process not a destination.
The process is:
- Assessment – What is working and what is not.
- Goal Setting – Choosing what to change. Setting priorities.
- Feedback--Measurement and re-assessment.

How do we promote positive change?
We grow by being a prudent "gatekeeper." Everyday there is a parade of information, images, sounds and people that want entry. It is as if our soul is protected by a series of walls, each with a gate. If we open all the gates or keep all the gates closed, we have unhealthy borders. Our personal protocol for opening (or closing) gates determines the rate and kind of growth. We

need training in "gate-keeping skills." We want to be a person who keeps opening our gates to others. We want to be person who keeps opening gates to God's Spirit until he is to the very core of our soul. This is what personal growth means!

TOPIC #9
What Abundant Living Is

Coming to the point of believing in Jesus Christ as Lord and Savior is a milestone on the journey, not the destination. It is the point where we are assured of eternal life with Christ, where the Holy Spirit takes residence and where an abundant new life begins.

Abundant living is not a life of carefree, six-pack happiness, but an enduring joy. It is true that living a godly life and having the divine protection of God spares us some of the pain and anxiety of this fallen world, but not all of it. Mere happiness is conditioned by external circumstances, but joy is an inner quality of mind and emotional well-being. Based on the assurances of scripture and the indwelling of the Holy Spirit, we can experience true enduring joy regardless of circumstances.

JOY is knowing God is sovereign and has ultimate control.
JOY is knowing God knows, understands and is always there.
JOY is knowing God's grace and forgiveness.
JOY is knowing God can even use our mistakes for good.
JOY is knowing God forever no matter what happens.

Experiencing joy is abundant living.

TOPIC #10
What Drives Us?

What motivates us to do the things we do and how do we feel about what we have done? We have within us varying degrees of physical, emotional and spiritual energy that needs an outlet. One of the challenges of life is to build up and to focus each one of these energies to accomplish abundant living.

We have a basic human need to satisfy our outlet for our energies.
The need may be:
>   1) **Pride – "I can do it by myself."**
>   2) **Obligation – "should have's" or "ought to's"**
>   3) **Pleasing others – "that-a-boy's"**
>   4) **Self-approval – "I can do everything."**

The alternative is to direct our energies into enjoying life and accomplishing the truly meaningful things, so we can ultimately say, "Mission Accomplished, Sir," and hear, "Well done my good and faithful servant."

What is the process that takes us from the treadmill of human "drivenness" to abundant living? The process begins with accepting ourselves as a fallen, limited creature but still valued just as we are by God, others and ourselves. The next step in this process is creating Life Goals. This is the life changing process that God can use to determine what is truly important and significant for us. The final step in the process is to establish priorities based on our goals. Living by priorities focuses our energies. Priorities without goals mean everything is a priority and trying to do everything exhausts all three of our energies.

Living by priorities means getting done each day those things which fit your established priorities and leaving the rest to others and God. Having a profound sense of priority means ending each day with a sense of accomplishment and not feeling guilty about what is not yet done. This leaves some margin in life for rest and enjoying the non-priorities. Being constantly busy exhausts our physical bodies, dulls our spiritual senses and saps our emotional energy.

Prayerfully put your goals and priorities in writing and begin an abundant life worth living.

TOPIC #11
Spending – A Lifestyle Issue

There are three things that you can do with your money: spend it, gift it or save it. Spending is a lifestyle issue. Spending should be whatever remains after saving and gifting. Spending is the part of your life plan that supports your lifestyle.

The first step is to prepare a budget making a list of all your expenditures and group them by category, e.g. all utilities together, and then total.

If your income after taxes, gifting, special projects and saving is sufficient to fund your total budgeted expenses, then you need to review each budget item or category to assure yourself that you are spending money where it will benefit you the most.

If the net available is not sufficient, then you need to aggressively scrutinize each item and establish a minimum but realistic amount until you are in balance. It may be possible to defer or freeze expenditures until income rises to reach balance.

If the net available is not sufficient after scrutinizing each expense, then you need to change your lifestyle. This is almost always a difficult emotional decision and a difficult one to live with, but in the longer term it will pay off. This decision is often the result of a divorce, a loss or change of job, discontinuation of a second income, the death of a spouse, or a financial setback. Sometimes a change is needed because of an unrealistic lifestyle that is underwritten by debt. It may require changing houses because it is the largest expense and tends to drive other costs.

Another aspect of lifestyle is your home. Homes are usually a good investment and tax shelter but your lifestyle needs should be the primary basis of your decision-making. In the ordinary course of life, typically your lifestyle needs will change every five to seven years. Do not ignore this and over-stay! Plan on paying off your mortgage by the time you expect to retire.

TOPIC #12
Gifting – A Heart Issue

God so loved the world that he *gave*....

An overflowing heart produces an overflowing mind-set, which produces an overflowing life, which produces overflowing giving to others. Gifting to others is inherently good because it is imitating a loving God whose very nature is to give. Gifts are intended to create good just as God is the giver of good and perfect gifts. Gifting is a heart issue because the Divine gifting process always begins with the heart. There is joy in heart giving. The mind-set of a giver is to be a good steward. Part of being a good steward is prayerful budgeting for designated amounts that provide strategic purpose and maximum impact. A mind-set giver has a well-ordered life. Mind-set giving provides satisfaction. The lifestyle of a giver is to be God's agent. As His agent we are always sensitive and alert for ways to appropriately minister. Lifestyle giving provides fulfillment.

Gifting can be done through sacrifice or flow from abundance. Gifts can take many forms: money, spoken words, written words, acts, things, listening, cards, prayers, e-mail, etc. A true gift can be an act of love, kindness, fun, compassion, worship, benevolence, encouragement, recognition, sharing, celebration or affirmation. A true gift is not given out of duty, obligation or social custom. A true gift is a valuable, unselfish and unconditional expression without thought or expectation of reciprocity. A gift is agape love in action.

The Divine paradox is that the giver benefits just like the recipient, and in the process, God is glorified. The recipient of a gift is thankful to God for the honor of being part of His royal family. Those who give more have more, and those who receive have more too. It is a win – win – win! Jim Elliot, a young

30

missionary to the Auca Indians gave us this wise insight: "He is no fool who gives what he cannot keep, to gain what he cannot lose."

Pray to be an overflowing imitator of God.

TOPIC #13
Saving – A Foresight Issue

There are three things that you can do with your money: spend it, gift it or save it. Saving is a foresight issue.

Saving is preparing for the future. It may be a reserve for the unknown or unexpected, or it may be for future special needs such as children's education or retirement. A good steward will usually save at a rate equal to at least 10% of what he spends.

The leading cause of financial failure is procrastination. Over 50% of American households will retire with an income of less than $35,000. America is a county where a person with an average income can accumulate a net worth of $500,000 or more through IRA's, 401K's, and equity build-up in a home. By world standards, a net worth of $2,200 will place you in the top 50%, $61,000 in the upper 10% and $500,000 in the upper 1%.

Because the other side of the savings coin is investing, you have the opportunity for your savings to grow. The longer the span of time from the date you save to the time you need the funds, the less you need to save because time and compounding do the work. Therefore, there is a great advantage in saving early in life (now) over later (tomorrow). In the planning process you can anticipate future needs, make reasonable investment assumptions and determine the saving rate required to realize your goal.

The reverse of saving is debt. Using debt for consumption or depreciating items simply increases the cost. Because consumer debt has high interest rates (10% to 30%), and because there is no tax benefit, it is best avoided. It is very easy to become trapped in a syndrome of having payments high enough to deplete cash and require further use of new debt. This can become a downward spiral that ends in a financial crash. Credit cards and other consumer debt are designed to entrap you by providing ready access to credit: "No Money Down And No Payments Until Next Year." They also allow low minimum payments and charge high interest rates so that balances can take five years or more to pay off. On the positive side, there is rapid progress in paying down the net principal balance earlier. Refinancing rarely solves the long-term situation.

Using debt for long-term, productive or appreciating items can reduce their ultimate cost. Using a mortgage to finance the purchase of a home is usually a good use of debt. It is important to know that debt is leverage and that leverage increases risk. The higher the risk, the greater the return required.

If you itemize your deductions on your tax return, you may be able to significantly reduce your income taxes, which will reduce the net cost of interest expense. Taxes can also have an impact on the net gain of interest income, depending on whether it is tax-free, tax-deferred or ordinary income.

TOPIC # 14
How to Make Right Decisions

Decisions, decisions, decisions! Life is nothing but a constant stream of decisions. From the time we get out of bed in the morning to the time we put our head on the pillow to go to sleep at the end of the day, there are thousands of decisions that have to be made. Most of them are routine or trivial, but some are important, like buying a new car, or really important, like whom we will marry.

How do we make good decisions or the best decisions or the right decisions? There are a number of systems and techniques available to help you understand the decision-making process. Try classifying decisions into these three categories:

1) The ones that can be made quickly and without a lot of thought--the routine or trivial. Those that do not make a big difference in their outcomes such as, do I order pie, ice cream or both.

2) The kind that require some thought but where time is working against you so they require a timely response, like when to leave a melting iceberg that is drifting out to sea.

3) The ones that require thoughtful consideration, but where time is working for you, so the decision can be delayed, such as when to bottle wine that is fermenting in a vat.

Wise decision-making is looking forward to see the long-term results or seeing life from the top down rather from the short-term bottom up. It is having the insight to see the unintended consequences of a decision. It is making decisions based on principles rather than pragmatics.

When we become a believer in Jesus Christ, our paradigm changes. We approach life from a different perspective. We become sensitive to a needy world.

The change is:

Me becomes you.
I becomes we.
Mine becomes His.
You means caring – respecting the needs of others.
We becomes community – rejoicing together when things go well and encouraging when things go badly.
HIS becomes stewardship – gifting of yourself.

Now you have the basis for making the right decisions.

TOPIC #15
How to Think Strategically

One way to live your life is one day at a time. These are people who take things as they come, enjoying the good things in life and coping when things do not go right. They love routine. They are easy to get along with.

Another way to address life is with pragmatism. These are practical people who do things right, get things done, and get the maximum number of things done every day. They are driven and very efficient, but at the end each day they have the feeling that they have not done enough. They may be hard to live with but are respected and sometimes admired.

A third way to address life is being a strategic thinker. These are people who know themselves, know what they want to accomplish, and what they want to do. They are not concerned with how much they can accomplish each day but with getting the right things done that move them toward accomplishing their goals. They are very effective. They are easy to live with, but pragmatists are frequently frustrated with them because strategic thinkers pace themselves.

Who is a strategic thinker? One who has a dream, an imagination, a goal and a vision of the future as well as strategic intent. This may be something new that has never been done before or just rearranging things that already exist. It may be very simple like Wal-Mart's "Always low prices" or highly complex like Apple designing and marketing an iPad. The idea must be clear in your mind. You must be able to express and communicate it clearly. This takes place with brain-storming and creativity. The secret to this is not to evaluate an idea at this point in the process but to keep building on it. It may seem impossible or at least improbable but that is okay.

American history has more strategic thinkers than you can name. Here are just a few:

First, the founding fathers – George Washington, John Adams, Thomas Jefferson and Ben Franklin – who conceived of a radical new form of government governed by the people. They expressed their idea in the founding documents. Their dream seemed impossible, but they sacrificed and won.

Seventy-five years later, Abraham Lincoln saw the issues clearly – preserve the Union and abolish slavery. He expressed his goals in a speech in Gettysburg, Pennsylvania: "A government of the people, by the people and for the people... All men are created equal."

Martin Luther King saw things differently. In his speech "I Have a Dream" he explained the need to end evil segregation. From the end of the Civil War it took another 100 years for Black people to fully enjoy the freedom of the American dream, but King made it happen by his non-violent civil disobedience strategy.

Jack Kennedy inspired the country with his challenge for men to reach the moon within 10 years.

Ronald Reagan ended **the Cold War without firing a shot** by his Star Wars idea. He expressed it in Berlin: "Tear down this wall."

Oprah Winfrey became one of the wealthiest women in the world with her idea of a TV show and pyramiding it into a giant media network. Each of these people had an idea, a dream or a goal and was able to cast the vision in such a way that people could understand it and own it.

Once you have your strategic intent in place you can move on to **strategizing**. This is determining how you want to accomplish your goal. It is done by thinking of as many ways as possible that you could accomplish it. It is trying out various scenarios. It is asking the "what if" questions. You may have some facts, but there are so many variables. Who can know the future? There is nothing more uncertain than tomorrow. You will intuitively know which option should be your first try, but it may require more than one try. If the strategy is not right, the execution will not succeed no matter how hard you work. The book and movie *A Bridge Too Far* about the invasion of Europe during World War II, tells of faulty strategy where American soldiers tried to take control of the farthest sixth bridge without success, despite heroic effort. You will know if you have the right strategy because implementation will flow.

The last step is implementation, which is the **Action Plan**. It is a "to do" list. It is where reality begins. The list may need revision or additions as you move forward. Flexibility is required. It may be obvious where to begin, or you may have to just start making things happen. The list is where the Pragmatist begins by skipping the hard work of thinking things through. Intuition is the mental process of the mind coming to a conclusion with very limited information. It works well and we all use it. The Pragmatist substitutes intuition for the hard work of strategic thinking because he thinks it is unnecessary.

Being a strategic thinker is a way of life. It is doing life differently. It is doing life intentionally. It brings meaning and significance into your life. Being a strategic thinker is not for everyone. Your basic temperament or ingrained thinking patterns may block it out. But almost everyone can benefit from this approach to life. The exception is the Pragmatist whose mindset blinds him from understanding this concept because he is too preoccupied doing things. That is all right because the world can always use more doers.

38

TOPIC #16
Understanding Yourself and Others

Have you ever thought about how you live your life and how you make decisions? While we are all unique individuals, we tend to fall into one of four general categories--leaders, builders, actors, and artisans. While more sophisticated classifications of personality are available today, this more classic categorization will do for our purposes.

If life is like a grid, how does each personality category view it?

Builders
The builder sees the grid as a matrix with an unlimited number of rows and columns like an Excel spreadsheet. Data is entered into each square and then analyzed. There is no problem that cannot be solved with this method. These are the people who design and build things. As students, because of the way their brain processes information, they frequently excel in math and science and they consider courses that require a lot of reading to be boring. These people typically have occupations like accountants, engineers, actuaries, cooks, or construction and industrial workers. They are problem solvers and builders of things. They deliver goods and services.

Leaders
The leader sees the grid as a chessboard with all the pieces in place. The game is played by strategic moves to checkmate the competition. The object of the game is to win. These are people who build organizations. They are strong-willed and independent thinkers. These people are typically entrepreneurs and have occupations like business executives, government officials, military officers, athletes, or attorneys. They are the builders of the culture.

Actors

The actor sees the grid as a stage where they are the only character. They will sing, dance, and speak their part to influence the audience. They are communicators. These people have occupations like actors, salesman, marketers, magicians, pastors, evangelists or music directors. They are change agents of the culture that make things happen and make life fun.

Artisans

The artisan sees the grid as a patchwork quilt with each square an array of contrasting or blended colors. The alignment of the patches creates lines that are pleasing to the eye. This arrangement makes the piece interesting. These are the creative ones who can think outside the box but lack organizational skills. These people care about others. They love animals. As students, because of the way their brain processes information, they frequently excel in English, the arts, and social studies courses but struggle with math and science. These people typically have occupations like artists, musicians, architects, interior designers, counselors, chefs, nurses, and teachers. They are the people who enrich our lives.

* * *

Leaders and actors are self-centered.
Artisans and builders are more concerned about others.

Leaders and actors are more assertive.
Builders and artisans are more passive.

Leaders and builders are fact-and-reason decision-makers.
Actors and artisans are intuitive and emotional decision-makers.

Leaders and builders are oriented toward things and ideas.
Actors and artisans are people-and-relationship oriented.

Leaders and builders are planners.
Actors and artisans take one day at a time.

TOPIC #17
Are Relationships a Priority?

The Creator matched people and time to a 24-hour-a-day cycle. That means having a full life is filling each day to the maximum with as much activity as our body and/or mind can endure. We get more efficient with time management, using technology and sleeping less. We leverage our time by using others and substituting money and things. The culture's concept of "relationship" is known as *networking*--a socially acceptable way of using people to our advantage. Americans know how to use their culturally generated anger to produce a sustained elevated level of adrenalin. This creates the motivation and energy to get things done but leaves us chronically fatigued and relationally bankrupt.

Biblical living uses a different paradigm. It focuses on the quality use of time, not the quantity of activity. It places the highest value on the person, and therefore, on personal relationships. Our relationship hierarchy is God, people and things. With wise, godly priorities we accomplish what is truly important. That requires leaving margin for the people in our lives. It is difficult, or even counter-productive, to be efficient about relationships. Relationships require time, TLC and mutual cultivation. As believers we use our God-given anger to motivate and energize ourselves to be more efficient at chores and tasks, but we direct that same anger to motivate and energize healthy authentic relationships – giving more than we get. Things eventually pass away and all that endures are relationships. Relationships make our life meaningful and make a significant impact on others.

The question is, are we a product of the culture or a product of God's workmanship?

41

CULTURAL INSIGHTS

TOPIC #18
A Worldview that Makes a Difference

Are we just a speck in a vast universe measured in light-years and a mere instant in eons of time? Are we no more than a temporary state of consciousness, a stream of hormones, a blip of energy and a future limited to no more than passing on our genes? Or are we, as the Bible says, the special creation of a personal God? Does what we do on this planet have meaning and significance which carries eternal consequences?

In order to live life well we need to have a perspective or an overview as a context for decision-making. It is how we keep life in focus. That is best captured as a *worldview*. This means we have to have a firm fix on the world as it really is and an understanding of how things work.

A *worldview* has to address three basic questions:

1) Origin – Where did all this come from?

2) Meaning -- Why are we here?

3) Destination -- Where are we going in the future?

We probe space to explain things with a "big bang" that occurred 14 billion years ago when matter, energy, time and measurement began but ignore what caused the bang. We try to explain life as an accident of lighting striking a prebiotic soup 4 billion years ago, but can't prove there was any soup. We try to explain the orderliness and function of life as a result of random chance over ions of time, but can't bring ourselves to admit the reasonable possibility of an Intelligent Designer or Creator. We try to ignore that earth is a unique and only planet in the entire universe where life can exist. Now scientists, whose minds are clouded by ideology, look to astrobiology for the origins of life because the earth's origins do not fit their theory.

We confidently declare that all lifestyles are morally equal, but are at a loss to explain the consequences of evil, good, and where it might have come from. Is it reasonable to believe that morality came from an amoral evolution or from God's nature? We declare life as temporary, subject to arbitrary termination, but have no remedy for the meaningless, purposeless, hopeless mental state this worldview creates.

The Christian worldview, as described in the Bible, is the only view that gives an adequate explanation for all three basic questions. The sooner we have insight into the scriptures, the sooner we begin to have a framework on which to build our worldview.

Without a worldview, we are like the bewildered middle truck driver in a three-truck accident. Based on fact he can be pragmatic and blame the truck driver in front of him or the one behind him, without ever knowing the source of the accident or its full consequences.

One of the things we do every day is to button our shirt. If we get the first two buttons buttoned right, the rest tend to fall into place. If we get the first two things in our lives right, a personal relationship with Christ and a Biblical worldview, the rest of things in life will tend to fall in place.

Most of the learning we do in life is either academic or experiential. This is primarily a bottom-up learning process. Imagine, for example, you get a new puzzle with thousands of pieces, and proceed to try and put it together. This might be fun, except that in this case the top of the box that has the complete picture of the finished puzzle is missing! Through endless trial and error, you may eventually get it right, but not without a lot of frustration and wasted time.

What the Bible offers is the global far-horizon top-down worldview. The earlier in life we acquire the big picture view, the better. Then, the rest becomes an adventure expanding our borders and filling in the blanks of life's big questions. All truth is God's Truth wherever he chooses to reveal it.

This is our opportunity for a life well lived with meaning and significance. The following insights are my adventure.

TOPIC #19
Before Genesis

God is sovereign and he does anything he desires in his own way. The following is my interpretation of how he did it.

Before the beginning there is an all-powerful triune God. God is a spirit with attributes of light, intelligence, holiness, goodness and personhood.

God uses the power of his light and with a single bang creates the cosmos with its atom based matter, dark matter and dark energy. Ordinary Matter makes up only 5% of the cosmos and can be seen, while super symmetric particles of Black Matter is 25% and cannot be seen (detected by its gravitational influence on visible matter) and Dark Energy is 70% and is the inflationary force that keeps expanding matter into intergalactic space. It is the gravitational forces of ordinary matter that pull matter together to form stars and planets. The gravity forces are constantly forming new stars from the light and radiation of existing stars but when a star reaches its saturation point it explodes into a gamma ray burst called a supernova. This scatters matter back into the cosmos to form new stars. The universe is expanding at a faster rate now because the initial thrust, black energy, of the bang is over-powering the power of the gravitational forces.

Albert Einstein (1879-1955), who believed ideas come from a super personal God, uncovered the relationship of energy, mass and light which has enlightened us as to the origins of the universe with his $E=mc^2$ formula (or light = square root of Energy/mass). At first Einstein believed in the conventional eternal existing universe theory but his observations of nature led him to the Big Bang theory.

In 1929 Edwin Hubble detected the first evidence to suggest an expanding Big Bang universe. Working at Mount Wilson Observatory he found that the galaxies in the night sky were receding at rates proportional to their distance. Running the clock backwards, this suggested that they had once emerged from something like a Big Bang. He discredited the theory of an eternally existing universe with fixed stars in space. The Bible states that God stretched out the universe in an ongoing process.

This is how God was able to create the universe out of nothing with light. With the event of the big bang 13.7 billion years ago, time and measurement came into being. Because light has a constant speed of 186,000 miles per second it is the primary measuring tool. Before the bang God eternally existed and that is the only plausible explanation of how something was made from nothing (John 1:1-9).

We are bound by time and measurement but God exists in an eternal state. The following illustration will help us comprehend how this can be. A few years ago Nate Saint brought the chief of the Auca Indians to the United States. In the jungle the chief lived in a timeless environment where each day was basically the same--sleeping, eating, hunting and gathering. Since time didn't matter he could do these things whenever he pleased. There was an endless stream of day and night, sun and moon and no seasons to measure time. It is as if he lived in an eternal world. But when he came to the U.S. he entered a culture where time means everything. The time we are born becomes the starting point for when we may enter school, vote, drink, collect Social Security, etc. There is a time when we get up in the morning, arrive at work, eat lunch, go home and go to sleep. Even our brains are programmed into a sleep/awake cycle. We even take time management classes to help us manage our time better. We are in a time-bound environment. This is how a time-bound world and timeless eternity can co-exist.

Out of the billions of galaxies with 70 sextillions of stars, God created one privileged planet about 4 billion years ago. With so many stars you would think that there would be a high probability that there that would be other planets like ours, but there is no other planet like it in the universe, and it is futile to try and find one. (God created the heavens and *the* earth.) The earth was precisely positioned to orbit 93 million miles from its sun/star to provide the temperature and environment to support carbon-based life with water, which is unique to the entire universe. He caused an asteroid to collide with the planet and with the great impact to throw enough debris into space to create its own orbiting moon 238,000 miles away. The moon with its gravitational force produces ocean tides which are critical for our earth's temperature and environment. Then 3.6 billion years ago God began the creation of life with the building blocks of DNA, genes, amino acids, enzymes and proteins and with the ability to reproduce its kind and adjust to its environment.

Genesis 1 gives an insightful description of the process of creating life one specie after another. (The controversy over whether it is six 24-hour days or six periods of time seems to me to be irrelevant since God with his supernatural power could do it either way.) Finally, God created humankind reflecting some of his own attributes--the ability to reason and an eternal soul. It is this quality that gives human life dignity and value above all the rest of creation. God created human beings with a neocortex larger than any of the animals and with the intuitive capability of language and music so we can know him and praise him.

By the end of the Middle Ages, European Christian thinking and science had surpassed that of the rest of the world, namely China and Islam. Because God was intelligent and reasoned, he created a universe that had order and natural laws. Because God had given men the power to reason, history was an upward progressive slope of uncovering God's design in nature (science) and discerning his will (theology), unlike other cultures that perceived history as an endless cycle. This premise motivated both the natural and social scientists to pursue knowledge and innovation. It also gave rise to individualism--personal accountability to God--and the work ethic--serving God. This power to reason led to individual freedom, property rights, entrepreneurialship, capitalism, and eventually to equality for women and minority races.

In contrast, Charles Darwin would erroneously theorize that nature was in chaos, driven by random, blind, and purposeless forces. Charles Darwin (1809-1882) was born to change the world, maybe more than any man since Jesus Christ. He changed the paradigm of science from unlocking the mysteries of God's creation, where a rational universe existed because God was an intelligent creator, to enlightenment of man's curiosity of the natural organic processes. He was a botanist who in 1835 sailed the seas in the ship *H.M.S. Beagle* to the Galapagos Archipelago in the Pacific Ocean. There he observed the changes in Finch bird beaks and concluded that, for all living things, change is necessary to survive in its environment. What he did not know is that the bird beaks reverted back to their original shape a few years later. It was not the strongest but those that could change that would survive. He then theorized that "natural selection" was a blind, purposeless, meaningless process that only the fittest could survive. He attributed the similarity of the genetics of different species as coming from a single source and as evidence of evolutionary development rather than as intelligent design. He mistook micro-evolution, adaptation within species, for macro-evolution. He theorized that mutations in the genes provided the basis of more and more complex life as it adapted and thrived. Mankind with its ten trillion cells was the result of thousands and thousands of years of evolutionary development, not a unique creation of God.

He documented his work and theories in two books – *The Origin of the Species* and *The Descent of Man*. Although he was coy about the applications of his theories during his lifetime, he clearly changed his late-Victorian Christian beliefs. The materialism/naturalism thinkers and activists immediately hijacked his science to give credence to their atheistic belief that God did not exist. Julian Huxley (1887-1975), a biologist, author, humanist, and atheist, observed the following about Darwinian evolution: "Evolution is improbable and un-provable but the alternative is unthinkable." They claim that they are objective fact-finder scientists but this is just a cover for their irrational godless ideology. Thus began a controversy that boils to this day.

Darwin's theories have significant weaknesses. They are:

1) Inadequate explanation of the origin of the earth
2) Inadequate explanation of the origin of life
   (He believed in "spontaneous generation" whereby a few chemicals combined to convert dead matter into molecules of plasma life. With the discovery of DNA in 1953 molecular biology has revealed that cells are not just matter and energy but also include massive intelligence. The single Amoeba cell has DNA with enough information to fill 1,000 sets of the *Encyclopedia Britannica*.)
3) Lack of evidence in the geological strata of the earth to show intermediate changes in species as would be expected by the natural selection theory
4) Inadequate explanation of "irreducible complexity" (Assume the order of the creation of the eye is: an eye socket, an eyeball, pressurized fluid in the eye ball, a lens, a pupil, a neural retina with 120 million rods, 6 million cones, 1 million retinal ganglion cells, amacrine cells and bipolar neurons, muscles and tendons to

51

control the eyes in synchronized movement, and an optic nerve to link it to the brain transmitting at 1 billion bits per second. Then how can each functionless step be justified as contributing to the survival of the fittest? Charles Darwin was well acquainted with the exquisite construction of the eye, the way the lens is perfectly positioned to focus light onto the fovea part of the retina, and the way the pupil adjusts the amount of light that enters the eye. The eye would be useless if it were anything but perfect. Darwin, in *The Origin of the Species*, wrote that the idea of natural selection producing the eye "seems, I freely confess, absurd in the highest degree." The eye being created in one jump is just as absurd.)

5) Inadequate explanation of how ethics and morality developed under a survival-of-the-fittest environment

6) Lack of common sense about what is plain (After 200 years of promoting Darwinian evolution, 90% of people do not accept it, 90% of apes, chimpanzees and biologists believe it!!)

If Darwin's theories had remained in the scientific community where they could have been challenged with honest debate, it would have been good, but they didn't. They infected religious and sociological thinking with the premise that without God, man would evolve into a utopian world through science. Francis Crick proposed the Panspermia theory that the first living cell must have come from some other planet outside our solar system. President Woodrow Wilson said that scientific materialism was relativity based on Darwinian theory: "Living political constitutions must be Darwinian in structure and in practice. Society is a living organism and must obey the laws of life… all that progressives ask or desire is permission… to interpret the constitution according to Darwinian principles." It affected crime and punishment public policy based on the conclusion that criminal acts were deterministic, involuntary and driven by our generic instincts of "survival of the fittest" rather than the voluntary acts of a corrupted and sinful mind. Therefore criminals should not be held responsible for their acts before man and God, and should be punished accordingly. It affected public policy to justify eugenics to upgrade the human species by sterilization of the racially and mentality unfit. In the first half of the twentieth century 36,000 people were sterilized, until the practice lost public acceptance.

Adolf Hitler based his "final solution" and select breeding programs to build a master race on Darwinian principles. It affected religion by forsaking the "sinners in the hands of an angry God" to secular humanism that could lift man to higher levels through education that would eliminate poverty and crime. New York justified the cost of building schools based on the idea it would avoid the cost of building prisons. It substituted a supernatural God of the universe with "higher criticism" thinking, and God's absolute Truth with situational ethics and relativism.

Today there is more scientific evidence for creationism than for Darwinian evolution. Intelligent observation of the universe and life leads to belief in God. But faith that Jesus Christ is the Son of God comes from accepting the Gospel account of Jesus' birth, life and death. John Barrow says, "Every molecule of carbon in our bodies originated in the stars," but only God can give it life. Aren't you glad you were created in the image of a supernatural God rather than coming from a choanoflagellate (microbe) that evolved into a monkey!

TOPIC #20
It's all about Family

It is all about family. God instituted family with the creation of Eve because Adam was lonely and needed human companionship. We have an innate need to be part of a relationship bonded by birth, marriage or adoption.

Family is so basic and important that the Bible has one whole chapter of Genesis, the first book of the Bible, and the first chapter of Matthew of the New Testament devoted to family genealogy. Two of the Ten Commandments deal directly with family relationships: "Do not commit adultery" and "Honor your father and mother." Jesus modeled this in his relationship with his earthly father and mother.

Why is family so fundamental to our well-being? Why can't be Lone Rangers? We need family to fulfill our need for an intimate relationship between a man and a woman. We need family to procreate children, to care for their physical and emotional needs, to model what it is to be a father and a mother and to pass on Christian core values that make a civil society. We need to give words of encouragement and deeds of kindness, not criticism, to our extended family of uncles and aunts, nieces and nephews, cousins and in-laws. We need family to provide a sense of belonging, to know that there is always someone who truly cares about us, no matter what, and to give meaning to life.

What happens when families are dysfunctional? Adam and Eve as husband and wife made a bad decision that affected their children. Cain killed his brother Abel. Joseph's brothers betrayed him. There is heartbreak just like today when husbands do not love their wives enough and wives do not respect their husbands enough and the marriage ends in divorce. When children rebel and do not honor their parents, this also brings heartbreak to the family. This is the time for families to act and react like families. That requires patience, forgiveness and prayer.

May God bless our family with loving relationships and spare us the disappointment, heartache and bitterness that come with a critical spirit and broken relationships. As we mature and become more supportive of one other, we come to realize it is all about family.

TOPIC #21
A Tree with Deep Roots

Have you ever wondered where you came from, your DNA, your family roots? What country did your ancestors come from, why did they come, when did they come?

When you reach age 40 you start to take an interest in your heritage because family starts to take on a new meaning with each passing generation. You may start building a family tree that may go back many generations.

I have traced our family of 1,500 relatives. I found English royalty back to the 1300's, a relative who was a sheep thief, a volunteer militia Indian fighter, and a Virginia slave owner! Some of my ancestors came to the United States in the 1600's colonial period and the 1700's revolutionary period and settled in Connecticut and Virginia. Later they migrated to Ohio, Illinois and Kansas. Others came in the great migration of the late 1800's and settled in Illinois and Minnesota. All came for economic opportunity.

What is a family? It is people related by blood, marriage or adoption. When an adopted child reaches maturity they may have an intuitive desire to find their birthmother. Suddenly they seem to have a burning passion to find their roots. I know of a family where the daughter had her birthmother walk her down the aisle at her wedding. Fortunately the real parents, even though they were hurt, understood their daughter's deep desire to recognize her birthmother.

But what about people who have no known relatives or cannot trace their ancestors, like the descendents of slaves whose ancestors were only identified by their given names in historical records? What about children who do not know their father due to death, divorce or rape? Or children who are adopted by a single parent?

Recently I met a new believer who told me his story of conversion. His face showed he had had a hard life but his bright eyes told a different story. His car had broken down and he had no money and no family that could help him pay for the towing service. The owner of the tow truck told him how he could be adopted into the family of God. He accepted God's invitation and became a child of God (John 1:12 & 13). With his adoption God became his father and his fellow believers became his family. Knowing our ancestry gives us a sense of belonging, a sense of security and insight into where we fit. It gives meaning to life.

Jesus had roots. The first chapter of Matthew gives his genealogy: fourteen generations from Abraham to David, fourteen generations from David to the exile to Babylon, fourteen generations from the exile to Christ. Jesus had both royalty and a harlot in his genealogy.

When the angel of the Lord came to Joseph and told him about the circumstances of Mary's pregnancy, he called him, "son of David" – not Abraham (Matthew 1:18 -25). This was a fulfillment of prophecy when Nathan had a vision where God told David his offspring would be the savior who would build an everlasting kingdom (2 Samuel 7: 11 -17). David was a benchmark in Jesus' ancestry.

The last time Joseph is referred to as Jesus' father was when Jesus was 12 years old and that was also the first time Jesus called God his father. It seems likely that Mary was widowed at an early age because of the silence of the Scripture about Joseph after that time. Also, at his crucifixion Jesus charged his disciples with the responsibility of caring for his mother. During his lifetime Mary is referred to as Jesus' mother many times and they had a close mother / son relationship.

The disciples, Peter, John and James, were like brothers to Jesus. At his darkest hour he wanted them close by. When praying to God the father in Gethsemane, Jesus called him Abba, which is an affectionate name like Daddy.

The wonder is that God's family tree is still growing. Every minute of every day someone accepts Christ and becomes an adopted son of God and a joint heir with Christ.

All believers have a father, a family and roots!

TOPIC #22
The Paradigm – Do you have one?

What is a Paradigm?

A paradigm is how you look at something. It is seeing something from a unique point of view. You can look at something in more than one way, like looking in opposite ends of a telescope, where the same object looks large or small depending on which end you are using. That is why two people can see the same thing and have different opinions.

For example, a caravan of five trucks is traveling down a highway at a high rate of speed, and the lead truck suddenly brakes. Each of the other four trucks crash into the back of the truck in front of them. The driver of the third truck only knows that he has crashed into the truck in front of him and the truck behind him crashed into him. From a pragmatic point of view, it is a three-truck accident and from his experience he is sure of it. A bystander sees a small child dash onto the highway and the lead truck brakes to avoid hitting the child, with each of the following four trucks crashing in a chain-like fashion. From a rational point of view, the bystander understands the cause of the accident and its ramifications and he perceives it as a five-truck accident. Because their paradigms are different their conclusions are different.

Your paradigm makes a significant difference in how you perceive yourself, your life experiences and the world. Compare how an atheist views life compared with how a Christian views life.

The atheist believes that life begins by the chance meeting of an egg and sperm, that life is about power and ideology, and that death is the luck of the draw. The atheist perceives power as

59

control over himself (I can do as I please), things (e.g. driving a car), money (everyone has his price), people (authority over spouse, children, subordinates, and citizenry) and over interests of his mind (the arts and science). Ideology, not facts, is the driving force in his life. The atheist sees death as the end, and there is no hope for anything beyond the present life. The pragmatist is by nature a critic, a skeptic, a cynic and a mocker because he sees ethics and morality as situational. We are born and we live and we die. Pragmatism is experiential. That is all there is because as a pragmatist he is sure of it, and to think otherwise is foolishness. To him life is a three-truck accident.

The Christian believes that God assembles the chromosomes at conception according to his Divine wishes, that God gives us the power to live our lives, that death is just a passageway to eternity with him. God's power allows us to care not only for our own self-interests but also to care for others. The Christian understands the real fallen world and Christ as the only hope. The Christian is rational because he sees the whole picture and therefore sees life like the five-truck accident.

Changing our paradigm is very difficult because our mindset is so fixed on pragmatism. When Jesus taught that we should love our neighbor as we love ourselves, that he who loses his life shall find it, and that the first shall be the last in his kingdom, he was changing the paradigm. This shift was the reason that today most people cannot grasp these truths. Even his disciples after three years under his teaching did not really understand. It is understanding the rational paradigm that makes us new creations in Christ and gives purpose and meaning to life.

TOPIC #23
The Whole Truth and Nothing but, so help me God

Healthy productive relationships require integrity. Integrity is the consistent practice of truth in what we say and do. In order to practice truth we need to accept God as the Father of Truth (cannot lie), Jesus as the teacher ("I tell you the Truth…") and practitioner of truth ("I am the Truth") and the Holy Spirit as the revealer of Truth ("...will guide you into all Truth").

To deny Truth is to deny the existence of God. Truth is the power of God. Truth is God's perception of reality. God is the source of all knowledge, understanding and wisdom. Truth is applied as facts, reason and principles that build the foundation for abundant living. Positive emotions are not truth but are warm feelings precipitated by truth. Jesus saw real need (truth) and was moved with compassion (positive emotion). Truth-telling, while risky, demonstrates honesty and ultimately expands borders to truly connect with others. Truth sets us free.

The antithesis of truth is a lie. Just as God is the Father of Truth, Satan is the father of lies. A lie is an attempt to deceive. Lies are a form of being deluded or insane. All sin is a lie and all lies are sin. All lies are destructive regardless of the motive or intent. Lies constrict borders and enslave. There are two kinds of lies-- those we tell ourselves and those we tell others. Both are destructive. We personally deal with lies through mental mechanisms like rationalization, sublimation, substitution, compensation, etc. It is our way of avoiding the realization of how sinful we really are. It is believing the lie that we are not so bad and that we can be successful at life without God. These deceptions keep us from confessing to God and enjoying the freedom of forgiveness.

Lies lodge in our memory and precipitate gridlock emotions like fear, shame, guilt, and worthlessness. These inhibit and can make us prisoners of Satan for years.

Why do healthy relationships make a difference? Fractured and limited relationships leave us lonely and angry. They distance us from others and, as Adam discovered, we need helpmates for better living. Fractured relationships leave us emotionally bankrupt with negative feelings as our conscience does its work. We miss the warm spot and comfort of free exchange which enriches as we see the work and workmanship of God in others. We miss the wealth created by open exchange with others where we each contribute what we do best and compound mutual benefit.

The realty of Truth and truth-telling alone is as hard as bricks. While bricks are the building block of life, sometimes they need the moisture of the tears of love to make them into clay suitable for the Potter's hand. That is why as Christ-like practitioners of truth we need to speak the truth in love.

TOPIC #24
Core Values

The term CORE VALUES is a term used to describe a phenomenon that goes back to the beginning of humankind but has only recently been developed into a useful working tool. Almost every person, family, organization and people group has at least one core value.

CORE VALUES are those shared virtues that surpass all others in importance, meaning and significance. They define us and tightly bond us. Because they are esteemed as being of the highest worth, they cannot be compromised. They are the "Ten Commandments" of the Bible, "silence" of the mafia, "good deeds" of the Boy Scouts and "fidelity" in marriage. A Core Value can be as simple as Thanksgiving Day at the homestead where Grandma cooks the turkey and Grandpa carves it; or making pancakes every Saturday morning; or attending every family wedding and funeral. Core Values are perceived virtues that supersede all other virtues and overcome all barriers.

A Core Value can be a positive thing--said, done, or believed, or a negative thing--never stated in words, never done in public and never acknowledged. It can be assumed, implied or appear in the form of traditions, taboos, codes or creeds.

Core Values cannot be borrowed, imposed or copied. They are unique and usually develop over time through broad acceptance. They are self-reinforcing and self-perpetuating. They feel good and right, even when wrong. Violating them is unforgivable and as serious as a broken sovereign treaty.

Core Values are a useful tool when they are defined and understood. If they are stated, people can quickly buy in or exit. Those values are a useful tool when they are understood.

Culture (e.g. business, church, family or marriage) can be created to prosper them and activities planned to enjoy them.

Core Values are never to be violated, unless you want to alienate yourself.

TOPIC #25
If it Feels Good ... Do it?

It seems that sexuality is the most driving, shaping, frustrating, demanding, energizing, complex and pleasurable force in our designed being. In our corrupted world, it is understandable how sex can be commercially exploited and why it can lead to our personal and society's destruction. One of life's basic challenges is the mental discipline, lifestyle choices, behavioral control and godly empowerment that channel the energy of gender into productive things and fulfillment.

A key insight is to focus on gender – masculine and feminine – as a part of who we are i.e. Our Identity! Gender is a "XY" male or "XX" female chromosome pairing which drives hormonal production of androgen (testosterone) and/or estrogen. The SRY gene which is locus on the Y chromosome, the hormone Mullerian-inhibiting substance (MIS) and androgen hormone dictate to the neutral stem cells to form male anatomical conformation. The female anatomy is the default anatomy. There is gender confusion of less than 1% where there is androgen insensitivity syndrome (AIS) produces other kinds of harmful and illegal sexual deviance or a "XY" person with a female anatomy (Dr. David R. Brown, "It," *Minnesota Monthly*, Volume 39, #6).

Gender is hormonal in that it influences mental development as testosterone starts flowing through the brain about 7 weeks after conception. Gender is also psychological through cultural conditioning and reinforcement. Consider that Adam was a complete whole gendered person before Eve was created. Eve was a complete, whole, uniquely gendered person upon creation. You are a total complete person notwithstanding sex, marriage and children. However, marriage, sex and children are proper heart desires. Our culture is so obsessed with sex it fails to comprehend gender as completeness and leaves most of the population feeling unfulfilled, psychologically devalued and sometimes gender confused.

The outward behavioral expression of gender to another is sexual activity. Biblical teaching is unique, from all other cultures, in specifying that sexual intercourse between a married man and woman is the only appropriate outlet for sexual activity. Whenever gender is expressed as sexual activity outside marriage it is unhealthy. Sexual activity within marriage is healthy, if it is implementing divine purposes. For thousands of years, people have unsuccessfully tried to separate sex from reproduction i.e. so called "safe sex." The one million abortions per year document the utter failure of this ill-conceived unhealthy fraud.

Being sexually attracted to a person of the opposite sex comes naturally, but loving them is hard work because they are wired so differently. Biblical marriage is the uniting of two unique and differently gendered persons into "oneness." Oneness is an unnatural state because it goes beyond the usual human subordination of ego, individualism and self-interest associated with friendship, companionship, partnership or socialization. Oneness is perfected in sexual intimacy that is the psychological, mental and physical exposing and giving of yourself without embarrassment for the complete benefit of your spouse. This bonds two into one. But it is unnatural because the male likes pop music while the female wants a long symphony. Cultivating the environment for "oneness" is a continuing and changing process throughout marriage requiring the joint effort of both husband and wife. The alternative, at best, is exchanging self-gratification.

Biblical marriage is the family setting for the raising of children. Each parent not only contributes an indispensable fifty percent of the chromosomes to the child, but each contributes an

66

indispensable fifty percent to continuing development by the modeling of various personality traits and gender traits. While the mother's continuing nurturing role is apparent from conception on, the ongoing presence of the husband/father, after initially contributing sperm, is so essential that in his absence God has promised special provisions for widows and orphans. God describes himself as "father."

Children need "Gender Education" not "Sex Education." Male children need to know what a boy is and what makes a man as contrasted with girls/women (and vice versa). We need to be very careful not to stereotype individual traits by gender, even though they typically cluster at opposite ends of the spectrum. God's nature, as revealed in Scripture, encompasses a full spectrum of traits even though he is characterized by the male gender e.g. God demands justice, a masculine trait, but dispenses mercy, a feminine trait.

Because gender equips us physically, chemically and psychologically for the dual divine purposes of marriage, the unhealthy outlets for sex have always beset the individual and corrupted society. These can be 1) individual behaviors – fantasy to psychological sex addiction (typically pornography for men and romance for women) and physical self-gratification; 2) heterosexual behaviors – physical engagement in fornication, adultery, polygamy, prostitution, rape, pedophilia, and "hooking up"; and 3) perverse and unsanitary behaviors – homosexual or heterosexual sodomy and the use of objects for restraint/pain. These practices are unhealthy because it only benefits one party and uses and humiliates the other. Sexual indecency is one of the few specified behavioral prerequisites to terminate a marriage in divorce.

We are complete in gender. Gender equips us through pleasure and a love relationship for *marital* sex and procreation to accomplish divine purposes of "Oneness." *Sex/procreation* require proactive mind/body control and lifestyle management both before and after marriage. Life is more abundant if you understand God's design and use His power to channel our gender traits into productive relationships and outcomes.

TOPIC #26
Words are Powerful

There is nothing you use more each day than words. You read them, write them, speak them, and even think in terms of words. Words are common. Yet words can be powerful when used in powerful sentences. Words express more than facts and ideas.

Let's go back in history to see why words are so powerful and how they are used in sentences.

75 years ago   President Franklin Roosevelt, on March 4, 1933, in his first inaugural speech: "We have nothing to fear but fear itself." A short sentence, but so powerful you still know it.

The people were fearful. The stock market crash of 1929 wiped out the investing class. The banks closed in 1932, wiping out the savings of the working class. Farmers were undergoing foreclosures and unemployment was triple what it is now. Roosevelt sensed the emotion that was gripping the people and helped them overcome it by identifying it. Words can describe, express, or create emotions.

150 years ago   Another president, Abraham Lincoln, on November 19, 1883, at the Gettysburg Cemetery dedication: "Four score and seven years ago our fathers brought forth on this continent a new nation, conceived in liberty, and dedicated to the proposition that all men are created equal." A long sentence, but you still know it and many can recite the entire speech from memory.

Edward Everett, a well-known orator, gave the major address lasting 2 hrs, 8 minutes. Lincoln said more in 2 minutes and with 86 words than Everett said in 2 hours. Lincoln began his speech with facts and then went on adding information, reaching a grand conclusion: "All men are created equal."

250 years ago On July 4, 1776, Thomas Jefferson was ready with these words after the final draft of the U.S. Declaration of Independence was signed by 56 delegates: "We hold these truths to be self-evident, that all men are created equal, [and] that they are endowed by their Creator with certain unalienable rights." A long sentence of great wisdom.

It was a new idea that rights were given by God, not by the King or the government, and therefore, they were unalienable or could not be withheld. A long sentence expressing a profound idea.

2000 years ago Jesus Christ taught: "In my Father's house are many mansions" (John 14:2). A short sentence with impact.

Can't you see yourself passing the pearly gates, walking up the gold paved street, to your mansion? Words allow you to use your imagination.

3000 years ago King David in Psalm 23: "The Lord is my shepherd I shall not want. He makes me lie down in green pastures, he leads me beside quiet waters." A long sentence of poetic verse.

With your mind's eye you can see the shepherd with his sheep grazing and drinking from a pond. Words paint pictures.

4000 years ago Moses said to Pharaoh: "This is what the Lord, the God of the Hebrews, says: 'Let my people go'" (Exodus 9:1). A short sentence of defiance.

These were the words to a hard-hearted ruler. It was a call to action.

Sentences Are Powerful

Short sentences make a point. Short sentences make an impact. Short sentences have punch. Medium-length sentences carry the message to your reader. Long sentences keep adding information, leading to a conclusion or to a climax. It is word selection and sequence, not the length, which make sentences work and be powerful.

71

TOPIC #27
Life isn't Fair!

Children learn life isn't fair at an early age. Adults still struggle with fairness but at a more serious level. Why does a young mother who is needed by her three small children die of cancer? Why can't a young married couple that long for a family get pregnant when an immoral irresponsible woman gets pregnant and has an abortion? People are not fair, business is not fair, government is not fair, and life is not fair. Nothing seems fair!!

Fairness is the popular notion of our culture that life should be evenhanded. Somehow we should all benefit about the same. Politicians love to use the term "fairness" because it means whatever the listener perceives it to mean so we all agree with him. One of the conundrums of fairness is that while implementing fairness to one person or group, we are unfair to another.

Life is not fair because God is seemingly not fair! But God is just. Justice means we all eventually get what we truly deserve. God uses the unfairness of life to test and shape us and reveal himself. That is how God uses *all* things--fair and unfair--for good outcomes. God is not the source of evil, nor does he tempt us with evil, but He uses our evil and the evil of this world for his just purposes. It was not fair that a perfectly innocent Jesus was put to death on the cross, but God used that to make those who accept the fact justified in his sight. If you are stuck on "fairness," pray for mercy. If you believe in justice, pray for faith.

TOPIC #28
Music to my Ears

There are four major forces in the world. They are:

1) The power of God
2) The power of Satan
3) The power of human will
4) The power of music

The Beatles came to the U.S. in 1964 and changed the course of human history. It was not what they said or what they did; they just played their new style of music using electric guitars and called it "Rock." It appealed to a rebellious generation and became the dividing line between those under thirty and their parents. Over the years Rock music has become accepted as a legitimate music form.

In order to have insight into today's music, you have to understand the evolution of music and see its continuous change. The early New Testament church introduced the singing of the Psalms, probably using Plainchant. Plainchant is monophony or a single sacred melody, without accompaniment, sung by a single person or by a choir in which each member sings the same part. By the 300's St. Ambrose of Milan wrote one of the earliest hymns, "O Splendor Of God's Glory Bright," which was sung Plainchant until it was scored in 1690. By the 4th century, Aurelius C. Prudentius wrote the hymn "Of The Father's Love Begotten." By the 6th century, Plainchant became known as Gregorian Chant, which is named in honor of Pope Gregory I. While he had nothing to do with its actual creation, he codified and standardized it in liturgical procedures, but it was not to be used in the mass. There is no regular beat and its rhythms are a function of its words. Any dance-like beat would remind people of their sexuality and would not be conducive to meditation and spirituality. Gregorian Chant evolved into Ambrosian and Galliean Chant. By the 11th century (900 to 1000 A.D.), polyphony was introduced with one person singing one part while another person sings another part. This allowed improvisation. This innovation required a practitioner to be able to read and write music which developed notation.

In the 1500's Reformation Martin Luther wrote "A Mighty Fortress Is Our God" and introduced congregational singing. The printing press produced hymnals. All of these changes were met with skepticism or outright hostility.

When the organ was introduced to the church service back in the 1600's, it had 5-inch wide keys, which needed to be pounded. It divided the church. It took a number of years for the organ to be accepted as an appropriate instrument for church worship services. Now it is drums and electric guitars that are questioned.

The 18th century was the Revival period or golden era of classical music with J. S. Bach, Handel, Mozart, Haydn, Mendelssohn, Beethoven, the symphony, opera, the orchestra and performance. But even Beethoven caused an uproar when he broke tradition and wrote a three-part symphony rather than the accepted four parts. The 19th century was the golden era of hymns. Charles Wesley wrote "And Can It Be?" and over 8,000 other hymns.

In the 20th century we have an amazing variety of music performed by Irving Berlin, Rodgers & Hammerstein, George Gershwin, Tommy Dorsey, Louis Armstrong, Elvis Presley, George Beverly Shea, Canadian Brass, Beatles, Stevie Wonder and Michael W. Smith, just to list a few. Music has evolved over the centuries giving us a rich treasure and it will continue forever.

What is music? It can enter our mind as patterns of stimuli that produce feelings and meaning, and/or it can enter our soul as beauty. Soul beauty is always godly, but mind work can be godly or ungodly.

Why is music so powerful? It is because we use both sides of our brain when we sing or listen to music. The simultaneous stimulation of the right and left hemispheres of the brain means we involve both emotion and intellect, which facilitates learning and retention. That is the reason God instructed Moses to teach the people through song.

But how can we combine the forces of God and music? Rick Warren stated in his book *The Purpose Driven Church*, "The style of music you choose to use in your church service will be one of the most critical (and controversial) decisions you make in the life of your church." He said it might also be the most influential factor in determining whom your church reaches for Christ and whether or not your church grows. While a style of music may attract the crowds, it is music that is authentic worship that keeps them.

To stand the test of time, the music must complement the text, even if there are no lyrics.

So what should be our criteria for mind music, both in and out of church?

1) The lyrics should be wholesome and meaningful in terms of describing the human condition, conveying spiritual truth or story.

2) The music should take you in an upward direction and take you someplace. Symphonies always have a progression of three or four movements that introduce a theme and bring it to a climax. Hymns usually have a

progression. Some praise music just goes around in circles. Some Rock music gives me the feeling that I am going in opposite directions at the same time.

3) The volume of the music should be fitting and appropriate for the setting.

Most music passes these criteria! That is the point. We should be open and appreciate all types of music. God gives each generation an additional gift of unique music for our enjoyment and to celebrate his glory.

TOPIC #29
Morality and Optimism

Did you know that morality and optimism are linked?

Morality is a heart issue. Morality is doing the right thing. It is mimicking the virtues of God – love, peace, justice, mercy and the grace to forgive. It is following God's command – do not lie, cheat, steal, commit adultery, or lust after things. Furthermore, it is loving one another, and caring for the hungry, the sick, the disabled and the poor.

You are created by God to be good. Everyone has some good. Theologians call this "Common Grace." But when man was disobedient to God evil entered the world, thus a struggle between good and evil.

Morality is a mind issue. Moral people are not naïve and realize that they live in an evil world. Most moral people live better, more meaningful and productive lives. Their conscience gives them a moral compass. They see life as a glass half full rather than half empty. They believe they can make a positive impact on the world. They are positive thinkers. They are optimists.

Be a moral person; be an optimist? The choice is yours.

TOPIC #30
Are you Angry?

"No, not me, I am fine."

This is a typical answer you might give. Yet it is unlikely to be true because the vast majority of us are usually in some state of anger. The reason is that anger is normal! God gets angry. He has made us to get angry.

Anger is a feeling that is the response to external stimuli, and therefore, a construct of the mind. Emotions are internal mind responses to a thought. Anger is a feeling response you experience when you are being hurt, are frustrated, encounter injustice or when a personal boundary is trespassed. It is a psychological condition that causes a physiological response that demands an outlet.

It is easy to identify the anger in a person who responds by going out of control, but anger is expressed in other negative (and positive) ways. It can show up as:

1) Physical symptoms (headaches, backaches, high blood pressure, etc.) that will eventually kill;

2) A critical spirit toward others (legalism, perfectionism, blaming, controlling etc.) that will eventually destroy; or

3) A critical spirit turned inward (depression, worry, unworthiness, victim thinking etc.) that paralyzes and distorts life.

We respond negatively because our fallen nature predisposes us to sinful responses. This compelling negativity tends to become a very deeply entrenched pattern. The use of anger as a device

78

to manipulate or divide is rampant at both the personal and cultural level.

Scripture tells us to be angry but do not sin because anger is a justifiable feeling, but under our control. As believers we need to be insightful and properly identify our anger. Then we can channel our energy and motivation into managed positive responses.

Managing anger is a cognitive thinking process of:

1) A controlled response
2) Prioritizing for focus
3) Taking ownership of our own inadequacies
4) Being positively proactive in service or ministry

As believers we need more than anger management. Healthy relationships and joyful living require copious applications of God-type forgiving grace for others and for ourselves. Jesus, while on the Mount of Olives, experienced the emotion of anguish that was uncontrollable and therefore not sinful. After being unjustly convicted, cruelly punished, deeply humiliated, utterly rejected and nailed to a cross, Jesus managed his feeling of anger and said, "Father, forgive them, for they do not know what they are doing" (Luke 23:34). Thus, good triumphed.

Pray for the Spirit's power to be very angry but not to sin.

TOPIC # 31
What we Believe Makes a Difference

Liberals are driven by ideology and a desire for fairness and compassion. Conservatives are driven by individualism, facts and a desire for justice and liberty.

Conservatism and liberalism are not to be confused with the Republican and Democrat political parties. Although most conservatives are Republicans and most liberals are Democrats, there is a lot of crossover. Secular-Progressives are all Democrats.

Conservative thinkers are fact finders. This knowledge is used as the basis of understanding how things work. Understanding can be applied as wisdom. Conservatives deeply feel that their belief system is superior because it appeals to the mind. That is why I am a conservative. It is this conviction that drives the conservative to action. Conservatives who are Christians have core values of grace (Ephesians 2:8-9), biblical standards (Exodus 20:1-17) and lifestyle standards (Ephesians 4:17-32). They believe the purpose of education is to acquire facts--truth--and critical thinking skills. That is why conservatives are traditionalists who believe history is important to understanding the present and shaping the future.

Because conservatism is so mentally challenging, conservative talk shows have a basic appeal. Consider the daily conservative radio talk shows hosted by Dennis Prager, Laura Ingraham, Dr. Laura, Bill O' Reilly, Michael Medved, Bill Bennett, Rush Limbaugh, Sean Hannity, Michael Reagan, Ann Coulter, and Glenn Beck. Because family, education and career are the highest priorities, most conservative action is done through organizations with a broad constituency base for financial support and with strong leadership.

Liberal thinkers are idea-minded. Their ideology is a deeply held belief system that has unique social and political goals enacted through government, where selected facts--or no facts-- can be used to support their position. Their ideology never is about economic growth and development and is frequently un- economic. Liberals who are Christians have core values of community, love (I Corinthians 13) and comfort (Psalm 23). Their position on issues can be contradictory because each issue stands alone. For instance, the National Education Association (NEA) and American Association of Retired Persons (AARP) stand for abortion, which cuts off the very ones who will support them. Because liberal ideas are so elementary, they have little appeal for radio talk shows. After they get past the sound-bite clichés, labeling and attacking, they have little to say, as demonstrated by the failure of the Air America radio broadcast with Al Franken. Because they hold that all truth is relative (post-modernism), the purpose of education becomes instilling (their) ideas, diversity and tolerance.

Most liberal ideological action is implemented through political influence using governmental power and the educational system. That is why eighty percent of the professors in the Social Science Department of many universities are liberals. They have a small number of highly committed, super-wealthy individuals (George Soros and Peter Lewis) or foundations (Ford) for financial support. They have influence far beyond their numbers by effectively using a friendly media, by electing "politically correct" officials and by appointing judges who share their beliefs.

Ideas are more motivating than facts. Because politics is such a high priority, liberals have an advantage over conservatives. That is the reason why there are more aggressive activist liberals, while conservatives are more passive and think the facts will prevail. Unfortunately, there is frequently lots of damage done before the facts become reality.

TOPIC #32
Biblical Joy – It's Good Mental Health

"Rejoice in the Lord always. I will say it again: Rejoice!"
Philippians 4:4

The book of Philippians is one of the best mental health manuals ever written. The book's theme is joy or rejoicing. These words are used eight times in this short book.

Joy is not to be confused with happiness. Happiness is an emotion driven by circumstances while joy is an inner quality that even endures hardship. Joy is the mental state where we know God is in control so there is no reason to be fearful. Our outlook on life becomes more and more joyful as we mature in our relationship with God--when we see how he has changed our life, given us a kingdom mentality, and worked in the lives of those we know. Joy is a fruit of the Spirit – "Love, joy peace…" (Galatians 5:22). Jesus said, "I have told you this so that my joy may be in you and that your joy may be complete" (John 15:11).

Joy is more about trusting God than just being an optimistic person or being a happy camper. Our basic chemistry or DNA that determines our temperament is just a contributing factor. To be a Christian is to be a joyful person. If you are not, something is wrong.

Anxiety and its cousin Worry are the major obstacles to being a joyful person. Anxiety is being overly concerned about what is happening and worry is being concerned about what might happen. They are both mental conditions brought on by fear of the unknown. They may be real or imagined. They affect us physically and may paralyze us mentally so we cannot carry on with life's normal activities. From time to time we all suffer from them, but that is normal and healthy. When they overwhelm us we need help.

Paul has the right prescription for this problem. It is prayer (Phil 3:6). Prayer turns the situation over to God so we can have peace of mind. It is a peace of mind that affects both our thinking and our emotions. It is a peace that transcends human understanding.

How do we develop our minds to be joyful? We are to practice filling our minds with good thoughts: whatever is true, noble, right, pure, lovely, admirable, and excellent. Thinking about lies, revenge, malice, wrongs done to others or others have done to you, and impure or ugly things, evolves into sin, evil and depression.

Paul, the author of Philippians, says that he has sufficient courage to face the challenges of life or to even experience death (Phil 1:20). He does not dwell on the past but is a forward thinker with a goal (Phil 3:14). He shares his secret about how to live a joyful productive life. Regardless of circumstances, whether good or bad, we can accomplish anything because God gives us the strength. What is impossible for us is easy for God. It stretches us.

TOPIC #33
Biblical Joy – Joyful Living

You can be a joyful person if you are free from the guilt and shame of doing the wrong things. Doing wrong, whether it is one time or habitual, great or small, intentional or unintentional, is damaging to your body, mind and spirit. It takes the joy out of life. This is bondage, but forgiveness from these things sets you free for joyful living.

To understand how forgiveness works you need to understand *Grace*. Grace is complete, unlimited and final forgiveness. It cannot be earned, bought or deserved. Grace is a gift from a loving God who makes it available to those who acknowledge that they are wrongdoers and accept that Jesus is the Son of God who died on the cross to complete forgiveness. It applies if you are a young child or on your death bed. It is grace that sets you free.

How do you deal with guilt if you do not have grace? You cope through the use of mental mechanisms like rationalization: "I am not a bad person" or compensation: "I do more good things than bad." To the human mind, grace is counterintuitive. There is a human feeling that somehow I must pay for my wrongdoing. I may do it by repetitive prayer, reciting a mantra, or penitence – denying myself something or punishing myself. Some even punish themselves with a whip, while others may go into a trance seeking nirvana. This is bondage, not freedom.

Does grace allow me to do whatever I want because it will be covered by grace? Yes, but the key is, what do you want? After you become a believer and God is Lord of your life, Jesus has saved you from your wrongdoing and the Holy Spirit has entered your soul, then your wants change. You want to please God, to live a life of integrity, to love people more than things, and to care about the needs of other people. This is real freedom.

To us as Christians what happens when our wants or actions are not right? The Scriptures instruct us to ask for forgiveness from God. But aren't we already forgiven? Yes, but asking reminds us that God is faithful and can be depended on for complete forgiveness. It also causes us to reflect and resolve to do the right thing next time. This keeps us free.

People who want or delight in doing the wrong things are sick or evil. They are self-centered, uncaring or maybe even psychopathic. We know from the news media that murderers frequently kill themselves because they cannot endure the guilt and shame of what they have done. This is bondage.

God's grace is the bondage-breaker that sets you free and provides a truly joy-filled life.

TOPIC #34
Biblical Joy – Abundant Living

Jesus said, "I came that they may have life, and have it abundantly" (John 10:10b, NASB). Abundant living is having a meaningful and purposeful life. It is not about building wealth that can bring happiness but cannot produce joy. Having a meaningful life means impacting other people's lives. It is about building relationships. It is caring for people. Purpose means you have your priorities right and know what you want to accomplish with your life. This is abundant living.

We can start by having the right perspective on life. Are we just a speck in a vast universe measured in light-years and a mere instant in eons of time? Are we no more than a temporary state of consciousness, a stream of hormones, and a blip of energy having a future limited to no more than passing on our genes? Or are we, as the Bible says, the special creation of a personal God? Does what we do on this planet have meaning and significance which carries eternal consequences?

In order to live life well we need to have a perspective or an overview as a context for decision-making. It is how we keep life in focus. That is best captured as a *worldview*. This means we have to have a firm fix on the world as it really is and an understanding of how things work.

Before you can have a meaningful impact on others there are prerequisites. A meaningful life starts with you. Do you have a positive joyful attitude toward life and are you continuously growing intellectually, emotionally and spiritually? Do you enjoy new experiences or meeting new people? Are you a productive person whose life is in good order and do you have your priorities right? These are things you want to model as you influence people, care for their needs and share your spiritual journey. You need to have your life in good order so you have the time and energy to invest in them.

If building relationships is the means for a meaningful life, how do we do it? Think of relationships as a target with a bull's-eye in the center and a series of concentric circles. The bull's-eye is where you have the closest relationships. The outer circle is people you do not even know, which is most of the people in the world. The other rings in between are various degrees of closeness.

The bull's-eye is where you have the closeness of relationships or intimacy and the most influence--God, spouse, children, grandparents, parents, and possibly some friends. The next ring is people that are close enough to you that you know what is going on in their lives--close friends and relatives and members of your small group. The next ring is people you know, but not well enough to know what is going on in their lives--neighbors, co-workers, members of your church or just acquaintances. The final ring is people you do not know--the 7 billion people in the world.

The challenge for a meaningful life of joy is to move people closer and closer, ring by ring, over your lifetime. God's direction and timing are critical. The closer people are to you, the more impact you can have on them and the more impact they can have on you. Learning from others can enrich your life and make it even more enjoyable.

TOPIC #35
Freedom and Liberty

One of the factors creating American exceptionalism is the precise use of words by our founding fathers in writing the Declaration of Independence, the Constitution, and the Bill of Rights. They were well aware of the more than 600 years of history where men sought freedom and liberty from the dictates of kings. With this perspective, a unique understanding of the times and of human nature, they wrote about freedom and liberty.

We think of freedom and liberty as the same thing-- synonyms. But the founders defined them differently. Freedom was the right to do whatever you pleased. Liberty was freedom plus morality. Therefore, liberty was freedom constrained by doing what is right. They were very intentional in using these terms. John Adams said, "Our Constitution was only made for a moral and religious people."

The Declaration of Independence uses the word liberty rather than freedom. "We hold these truths to be self-evident, that all Men are endowed by their Creator with certain inalienable Rights that among these are life, **liberty,** and the pursuit of happiness." The creator intended us to be free, but also subject to morality that is founded in the Ten Commandments and the teaching of Jesus and the apostles.

The First Amendment to the Constitution, The Bill of Rights, gives us five rights. They were probably grouped together, rather than listed separately, because they are linked together so closely. Three are listed as specific freedoms. They are freedom of speech, freedom of the press and freedom of religion. The use of the word freedom means these rights are not encumbered in a way. We have the freedom to say whatever we want, to print whatever we want, and to worship God in any way we want. Note that it does not give us the freedom to do whatever we want. The founders did believe that each man was accountable to God, and therefore, it was safe to use the word freedom in these three areas.

Liberty was the paramount consideration. Patrick Henry expressed it well: "Give me liberty or give me death." The founding fathers knew from history that government by its nature always wants to control with laws and regulations and therefore needs to be constrained.

In our time when the lessons of history are so soon forgotten or ignored, it is critical to our lives, liberty and the pursuit of happiness, that we and the leaders we elect take careful note and heed the intent of the founding fathers who laid the basis for our form of government, sound in principle and of, by, and for the people.

TOPIC #36
Authority and Accountability

Americans have a distain for authority and accountability. We have been taught that we have rights and freedoms that we relish. But we have found that authority and accountability are necessary, if we are to be a prosperous nation. It is these things that are the glue that holds our nation, our culture, and our families together.

The use of authority is everywhere. God has authority over his creation, government officials have authority over the population, husbands have authority over their wives, parents have authority over their children, business owners have authority over their employees, and generals have authority over their troops.

But with authority comes accountability. Government officials are to rule justly just as God judges us justly. Husbands are to love their wives. Parents are not to be overly strict with their children. Business owners are obligated to pay their employees fairly, and generals are to care for the troops.

Those under authority are also accountable. Citizens are to obey the law, wives are to respect their husbands, children are to honor their parents, employees are to perform a good day's work, and soldiers are instructed to obey orders.

But what if authority is used for evil purposes or is abused? Then authority should be challenged, just as the colonials resisted King George's unfair taxes. Challenging authority is not easy but necessary.

Americans seem to have found a healthy respect for authority and expect there will be accountability. This is why we have freedom, order and prosperity.

SPIRITUAL INSIGHTS

TOPIC #37
Spirituality

What is spirituality? It is our capacity to experience the presence of God. It is thinking like God thinks and living it out in a Christ-like lifestyle.

But how do we find this way of thinking and living? The journey is: 1) seeking God, 2) finding God, 3) knowing God and 4) experiencing God.

Seeking God
There is a basic built-in drive that causes the human spirit to seek God. Sometimes it is an intellectual quest through logic and reason. Sometimes it is a scientific pursuit by seeing God in creation. Sometimes it is wanting to be a Christian because someone shares and/or models Christ. Or sometimes it is a void in life that lacks meaning that only a personal relationship with God can fill. If we seek God, we will find him.

Finding God
For the Holy Spirit to enter our soul it only takes a sincere moment when we give mental ascent to Jesus as the Son of God who died to cover our sin. It does not matter how much else we know, as we can see from the experience of the thief on the cross or from the experience of very young children or the mentally disadvantaged.

The Biblical teaching is that God finds us. That is, the Holy Spirit prepares our minds and circumstances for the encounter. It may be easy to accept the fact that there is a God, especially if we were taught that at an early age.

The fact that there is a God should be an "easy reach" when all you have to do is look around and observe the heavens and the earth, but it is not easy for many whose minds are closed and cannot accept it. They see evolution as a plausible alternative. But accepting Christ as the Son of God is a matter of faith. It is the Holy Spirit who gives us the faith to believe such an outrageous idea that God would send his son to earth to die for us. Most people think we are crazy, but those who are believers understand. The idea is so powerful that it makes us a "new thinker," thinking like God thinks, or a "new creation."

Knowing God

We can see God's nature in creation but we get to know him in the Holy Scriptures. God is a person, not human, but a spirit with a triune nature. God the Father is in total control, Jesus is God in the action function and the Holy Spirit is God's presence in the world and in our souls. As we mature, the Holy God of this vast universe transcends from a concept or a distant Spirit into an intimate personal friend and trusted companion. Faith is a prerequisite for believing, believing is a prerequisite for trust, but you can only trust a person you know.

Experiencing God

There are a number of gateways to experiencing God: worship, nature, service, intellect or a passion for some activity.

Letting God-thoughts flow though our minds enables us to act like Jesus and we don't have to doubt or test our motives. It is the confidence that God is in control of our lives and the world around us. It is praying to change the natural course of events. It is meditating on a morsel of Scripture. It is slipping into the silence of solitude to hear God whisper in our mind. It is experiencing the warm feeling of God's presence.

Praying becomes more than a monologue which is like direct electrical current where we just lift our thoughts and voices to God. But it is more like a conversation, like alternating electrical current, where you tell God your concerns and God fills your mind with his thoughts and direction.

TOPIC #38
God's Will for your Life

Have you ever wondered what God's plan is for your life? As a believer in Jesus Christ, is your desire finding and doing the will of God and is it a paramount priority in your life?

Is God's perfect plan like a jigsaw puzzle where all the pieces are designed to fit a perfect picture and where everything is predetermined? Or are you faced with the challenge to figure out how to put all the pieces in the right place and putting one piece in the wrong place makes your life a hopeless failure? Since this has you in an impossible situation, it must mean that God has a better plan in mind.

Think of yourself as a potter molding your life into a useful vase. You start with the raw materials. A body and mind with energy, intellect, emotions, talents, skills, and the will to manage them. You mold your raw material, creating something beautiful and useful, making mistakes but correcting them as the process continues. It is a dynamic process sometimes requiring you to start over again, but in the end you have a useful vessel. God plans the end result and helps in the process.

What is the molding process?

It is first using your God-given ability to reason. It is taking knowledge--facts and an understanding of how things work— and using it to make good decisions where you exercise wisdom (Proverbs 24:3-4). Most of doing God's will is using your mind to make wise decisions about both the small and the significant things hour by hour, day by day. These decisions need to be guided by the Holy Scriptures and with the Holy Spirit's leading. That is why the Scriptures urge you to pray for wisdom and you will receive it.

The next part of doing God's will is listening to God. It is the quiet voice in your mind that prompts you to do something. It is recognizing that a poignant thought that seems to come from nowhere is God's direction. It is feeling God's presence and approval. God is like your GPS that directs you to turn right at the next street and then keep to the left and then tells you when you have arrived at your destination. If you make a wrong turn, the GPS lets you know it is re-calculating to help you reach your destination by an alternative route. God will do that too.

The last part is God intervening in the ordinary course of events. It is God bringing someone into your life at just the right time or making you that right person for someone else. It is God protecting you from harm even though you may not know about the danger. It is God helping you to find the right doctor to cure your ailments. It is God helping you to find the right therapist to help you resolve your mental health issues. It is God sparing your life in a near fatal accident or giving you extra time on earth by healing you from your incurable disease. These are supernatural. These are miracles.

All good things are from God. We live in a sinful, broken and fallen world so all bad things occur with God's permission. But all things work together for good (Romans 8:28) because he uses the bad things to refine you, to help you desire God's will, to trust him more, or to prepare you for eternity with him.

TOPIC #39
The Ancient Words

Why should anyone still be interested in the ancient words of the Bible? Hasn't the explosion in knowledge and science surpassed the words of something written thousands of years ago? How can we trust words of scripture to be reliable?

To answer these questions, we must understand the historic origins of the Bible. The Bible is a collection of 66 books of rich complexity, containing a vast compilation of writings composed over 1,600 years by 40 authors in three languages on three continents and formatted into 31,173 verses.

By the fourth century the term Canon was the descriptive word used for the writings selected for what know as the New Testament and the Old Testament. The root of the word is a thick blade reed used to measure. For the Old Testament the primary measurements for selection were: 1) Does it claim to be of God? 2) Was it written by a servant of God? 3) Does it tell the truth about God, man, sin etc.? 4) Was the message internally consistent? 5) Was it consistent with the other canonical books? For the Old Testament, by 180 B.C. the Canon was established with 39 books accepted and 17 rejected. For the New Testament the criteria were that it had to have been written by someone who knew Jesus personally or was a contemporary of him. By 363 A.D. the 27 books had been agreed upon and by the end of the 4th century we had the Bible we have today.

The Old Testament consists of the Pentateuch which is the first ancient five books describing the origins of the universe and mankind, how sin entered the world and how the nation of Israel came into being. Then, there is the history of Israel, how God oversaw them through leaders and spoke to them through prophets. Finally, there are five books of wisdom interspersed in the text.

The New Testament begins with four gospels covering the birth, life, death and resurrection of Jesus Christ. Next there is the book of Acts, which describes the coming of the Holy Spirit and the beginning and spread of the early church. Then there is a series of letters sent to these early churches. Finally, there is the book of Revelation which describes how the world will come to an end. There are numerous books that are not in the Canon even though they were written by some of the disciples, prophets and apostles.

How do we know the scriptures have not been corrupted by copying errors over hundreds of years? The method of authenticating writings is to compare them with earlier copies. The Bible is by far the most authenticated ancient document. Over 5,000 portions of the New Testament have survived, in the study of historiography, thus making it as close to the originals as humanly possible (statically 99.2% accurate). But why didn't God preserve the originals? It may be that he knew the human propensity to worship tangible things that people can see which is idolatry rather than the invisible Spirit.

Compare this with the Holy Qur'an that Muslims believe contains the dictated words of God to a single person, Muhammad, by the angel Gabriel over a period of 23 years. Because Muhammad was illiterate he repeated the words to scribes who wrote them down and repeated them back to him for verification. The writings were compiled into a book after his death in 632 A.D. About 650 A.D. the Third Caliph ordered all of the more than 100 versions of the Qur'an to be assembled. He selected one to be the standard and ordered all the others burned or boiled. Therefore, there is no way to authenticate the book. Because most Muslims use Arabic, that avoids translation problems. While they all use the same standard version of the

Qur'an there are numerous interpretations. One of the most radical is the Al-Qaida sect's interpretation of the word "jihad" which they hold to mean "warfare with spiritual significance" against infidels (anyone who does not share their particular beliefs). The Qur'an invites Muslims to give their lives as martyrs in exchange for assurances of paradise.

The first English version of the Bible came from John Wycliffe (1320-1384) who translated the New Testament in 1380 and the Old Testament in 1388 from Latin. In 1415 he was declared a heretic for making the Scriptures available to the common people and his body was exhumed and burned, and his ashes scattered in a river. William Tyndale (1492-1536) translated the Bible into English from Greek in 1526. He was kidnapped and found guilty of heresy and burned at the stake. The organized church did everything possible to keep the Scriptures from the people. The church benefited from a "works and guilt" system and did not want the people to know about the Bible's "grace."

Does the Biblical text mean what it says and say what it means, or can it mean whatever it means to me? In the original documents it is Truth and means what it says. But in translations we need to interpret what it means and it becomes Truth. What it means to you is the work of the Holy Spirit guiding your thinking into spiritual truth that you can use in your life.

There are always challenges in translating the Scriptures from one language into another. Jeff Webster, a linguist, estimates he spent an average of 79 minutes on each of the 7,956 verses he translated into the Branchu New Testament. Here is an example of the problem. When translating the parable of building on a rock to a tribal people, you realize they live in a great desert and have never experienced a rainstorm. Do you use a rainstorm to illustrate the point because that would be a direct, word-for-word translation of the scripture, or do you contextualize it to be a sandstorm? Are you being true to what it says or what it means?

When I read the Bible, I read it for content--when, how, where, who--and the cultural context. I read it as literal unless it is obviously metaphorical. This builds a base of knowledge which provides a basis for the principles of life and a biblical worldview. I also read it as William Blake describes, seeing it though the "eyes of faith" searching for some morsel of Truth that I can mull over to know who God truly is and what he wants for me. The reason I have included some biblical background for most of my Insights is to show that it is not just my opinion or wisdom.

"Ancient Words" by Lynn DeShazo (1999) is a contemporary hymn worthy of thought.

ANCIENT WORDS

Holy words long preserved
For our walk in this world
They resound with God's own heart
O let the ancient words impart

Words of life, words of hope
Give us strength, help us cope
In this world, where'er we roam
Ancient words will guide us home

CHORUS:
Ancient words, ever true
Changing me and changing you
We have come with open hearts
O let the ancient words impart

Holy words of our faith

Handed down to this age
Came to us through sacrifice
O heed the faithful words of Christ!

Martyrs' blood stains each page
They have died for this faith
Hear them cry through the years
"Heed these words and hold them dear!"

TOPIC #40
Hope

What is hope? Is it just wishful thinking or is there more to it?
Hope is not to be confused with faith – belief and trust in God and in
the doctrines expressed in Scripture. Hope is the confident expectation
that some good will happen or at least things will get better.

Imagine you are sitting in a jail cell 6 feet by 12 feet. You will spend 23 hours per day, 7 days a week and 52 weeks per year for the rest of your natural life in that cell. You have no appetite for the three starchy bland meals delivered to your cell each day and cannot sleep at night because of the constant din in the cell block. The 1 hour time each day in the outdoor exercise yard is a welcome break from the oppressive boredom.

You have been wrongly convicted of a crime you did not commit and have been sentenced to life in prison without the possibility of parole. You cannot think clearly. Your mind is in turmoil – You rationalize –"Life is unfair, why me? Would it have been better to get a death sentence?" Your thinking is going in circles – "If only," "Could have," "Should have" dominate your mind. Your emotions are in turmoil – you are bitter, in deep depression and having suicidal thoughts. Your situation is hopeless. Without hope you want to die

While your situation seems hopeless, there is a slim chance that someday the evidence will be found to prove your innocence, there was an error in your trial procedure, the governor may commute your sentence, laws may change due to new court rulings, or you might escape. There is still hope. With hope your life has meaning and there is a reason to live.

Contrast this situation with how Apostle Paul, who was well aware of the Roman prison and justice system from personal experience, handled his prison experiences. After his third missionary journey he was wrongly accused and he was held in a secure Roman prison, a hole in the ground with only a small opening for fresh air, not knowing his fate.

But he was still a clear thinker. In his book of Romans he uses the word "hope" thirteen times. He produced a rational argument for believing in God and that Jesus Christ died on the cross for the redemption of mankind. The book is called the "Constitution" of the Bible. Paul was not just an emotionally positive person, but he rejoiced in hope--the confident expectation of spending eternity with the Person he met on the road to Damascus.

In Romans 5:1-5, Paul gives a strategy for using "hope" for dealing with our personal problems. "Therefore, since we have been justified through faith, we have peace with God through our Lord Jesus Christ, through whom we have gained access by faith into this grace in which we now stand. And we rejoice in the *hope* of the glory of God. Not only so, but we also rejoice in our sufferings [problems], because we know that suffering produces perseverance [patience for God's timing]; perseverance, character [building on our strengths] and character, *hope* [high expectations]. And *hope* does not disappoint us, because God has poured out his love into our hearts by the Holy Spirit, whom he has given us."

Our 30th U.S. President, Calvin Coolidge, gave us some wisdom on how to use "hope" as a strategy for our culture: "Little progress can be made by merely attempting to repress what is evil. Our great hope lies in developing what is good." God's plan is for us to bring good to our culture.

What is your strategy?

TOPIC #41
The Healthy Church

Every church has Core Values. What are Core Values? They are shared virtues that surpass all others in importance, meaning and significance.

Churches have choices. They can look back or look forward; they can look inwardly or look outwardly. Looking back is reminiscing about the past, it's about roots. Looking forward is vision, goal setting. Inward is introspection, strengthening and caring for the base. Outward is reaching out of your comfort zone, a Christian world view in action.

Churches that only look back and inwardly die! Churches that only look forward and outwardly lose their bearings and sense of belonging. They are like a rudderless ship running with its engines running full speed. While it is much better to look forward than backward and it much better to look outwardly than inwardly, a church needs a good balance. The church that does all of them well is healthy and thrives.

Churches that have pastors who are "shepherds" are especially vulnerable because the Core Value is caring for the flock. These pastors are well liked and loved by the congregation. They are expected to make home and hospital visits and conduct funerals. Tradition and sacred cows must be respected. They resist change because it causes strife in the flock. But this inward mentality eventually destroys the very thing they love, their church.

Churches whose primary Core Value is looking outwardly with every member committed to reaching their family, friends, neighbors, city, nation and world with the gospel message that God loves them are vulnerable too. These churches have pastors who are "cowboys" whose Core Value is rounding up strays and trying to brand them. Because their focused interest is out of reach, they do not develop the loyalty of their members and leave behind the core majority of people who are needed to support the work. These churches attract the entrepreneurial, non-believers, and people who are, or become, new believers. These people do not have the spiritual maturity or church background to lead the church. These churches are always having a shortage of teachers and wise leaders.

A well balanced church is a healthy church.

TOPIC #42
Power Play

Power and strength are synonymous. In our worldview there are three types of power:

1) Physical power
2) Emotional power
3) Spiritual power

God can provide all of three depending on the need.

Physical power is body strength. It may be the strength needed in battle, or to pull someone out of an accident or to stand up after surgery. It is strength for work and play and it is the strength that touches those who are suffering. It can be greeting a friend with a handshake or a fist used in anger. It may be the strength to endure or endurance to handle pain and suffering. Keeping the body healthy by good nutrition and exercise will build strength

Emotional power is "willpower" or mindset. It is the mental state known as "peace of mind." It is the "will to live" that can be the difference between life and death. It may be the fruits of the Spirit. It is the peace that comes when the doctor tells you you have cancer or the joy that eases the pain of losing a loved one to heaven.

Spiritual power is the supernatural work of the Holy Spirit. It is the power that comes into a person when they accept Christ. It is the power that removes the craving for drugs, alcohol, cigarettes or lust, which sheer willpower cannot overcome. It is the peace that transcends human understanding. It is the power to love the unlovable, to forgive sin, or to heal the broken heart or body.

Tapping all three will make you a powder keg!

TOPIC #43
Believing and Faith

We use the two words interchangeably. Believing in Christ and having faith in Christ are used to explain our salvation. But are they the same?

Believing is knowing something and accepting it as true. Believing is fact and reason driven. "To those who believed in his name, he gave the right to become the children of God" (John 1:12). Believing is knowing and accepting Jesus Christ as the Son of God and that he died on the cross to cover our sin.

People need to hear, know and accept the basic Gospel Message to become believers. "How, then, can they call on the one they have not believed in? And how can they believe in the one of whom they have not heard? And how can they hear without someone preaching to them?" (Romans 10:14) That is why we are mandated to go into the entire world and preach the gospel.

Faith is accepting something to be true without reason or direct evidence. Faith is something to be exercised after we have believed that Jesus Christ was the Son of God and have had the Holy Spirit enter our being. Faith is linked to grace. "For it is by grace you have been saved, through faith – and this not from yourselves, it is the gift of God" (Ephesians 2:8). Grace does not meet the test of logic. Why should God unconditionally forgive us for our sins? Don't we teach our children that if they are good they will be rewarded and if they are bad they will be punished? Most religions teach that if we do more good things than bad we will be rewarded. The concept of grace is illogical, so it takes faith to understand it.

Belief is a mental process requiring knowledge and understanding. Faith is an intangible. We need to grow in faith

106

by daily depending on the Holy Spirit to guide us, protect us and bless our work for him. We need to grow in faith by stretching ourselves with new experiences. Faith enables us to think and act outside the box. We need to do life differently.

Faith is accepting the fact that God is in control and that by praying we can change the ordinary course of things. This is the reason why we pray for people who are in hopeless physical, mental or other situations. Faith is dynamic and can be limited or unlimited. It can be present or absent. Faith is a gift from God.

TOPIC # 44
God on Redial

Excuse me for a minute; I need to make a call. I have called this number before so I have it on "redial."

"Hello, is this heaven? Is God available?"

He is always very good at making himself available when I call.

"I hope I didn't get you out of bed by calling so late…"

"Oh, that's right, there is no nighttime in heaven! Well anyway, this is Bob calling. You remember me? I was the guy who called with the wife problem…"

"Yes, things are fine now. I followed your instructions and everything worked out well. But now I have a mother-in-law problem…"

"Oh, you get a lot of calls about mothers-in-law, so you know how I should handle this situation. Good!"

"Oh, I know I could have avoided the problem if I had called before, but I thought I could handle it by myself. Things are pretty busy down here you know…"

"Yes, yes, I need to go to her and tell her I was inconsiderate and ask for her forgiveness…"

"I'll do it tomorrow. Goodbye."

TOPIC #45
Broken Relationships

"For God knows that when you eat of it your eyes will be opened, and you will be like God, knowing good and evil."
Genesis 3:4-5

Evelyn & Her Husband Have a Talk on Relationships

Husband: Now you have really fouled things up.

Evelyn: What do you mean "I" fouled things up? You thought it was a good idea at the time.

Husband: I should have known better than to go along with your stupid idea and it was your idea in the first place.

Evelyn: What are you going to say when the boss finds out?

Husband: What am "I" going to say? I am the head of this house and I say you are going to handle it. I'm going upstairs to watch the super bowl game.

Evelyn: Just like a man. Withdraw and disappear when it is time for accountability.

Husband: I have told you a million times, "Don't nag!" Things were going great until you came along.

Evelyn: Since it was the boss's idea that we be married, maybe we can come up with some way to blame him.

Husband: That will never work. I guess both of us are to blame.

Evelyn: Well, if that is the way you feel, will you forgive me, Adam?

Adam: "Forgive" is a new word for me. But if it will heal our relationship, I forgive you. Will you forgive me, Eve?

Eve: Yes, Adam, I would do anything to make our relationship what it was before.

TOPIC #46
Forgiveness

"Our Father in heaven, hallowed be your name, your kingdom come, your will be done on earth as it is in heaven. Give us today our daily bread. Forgive us our debts, as we also have forgiven our debtors."
Matthew 6:9 - 12

It sounds so simple. You just say, "I am sorry. Will you please forgive me?" and the other person responds with, "I forgive you," and that is the end of it. But in real life it may be very difficult to offer complete forgiveness or to accept it. When the words have been cutting and hateful or the actions have hurt deeply, it is only human to carry resentment or guilt. Unforgiveness and its counterpart forgiveness are facts of life.

What is Unforgiveness?
Unforgiveness is the harboring of ill will for some insult, lie, offense, hurt, misunderstanding, injustice, disappointment or injury--real or perceived--inflicted upon us by someone. We might even blame God. Unforgiveness is a delayed emotion involving resentment, bitterness, residual anger, residual fear, hatred, hostility and stress. These emotions are embodied experiences that are sending either chemical messages though our bloodstream that release hormones, or electrical messages through our nervous system to the association cortex. It is this complexity that makes it so difficult to deal with. It is not as simple as saying, "I forgive you." Good mental health is washing unforgiveness from your mind and body. We are "dishwasher safe." After we go through the wash, rinse and dry process, we are bright, shiny and clean from all the dirt and garbage.

111

What is Forgiveness?
Forgiveness is part of God's character and was exemplified in Christ's life when he prayed, "Father forgive them, for they do not know what they are doing" (Luke 23: 32). These were his first words from the cross. The soldiers had just driven the nails through his wrists and feet when he prayed this remarkable prayer. He had been beaten and humiliated, suffering pure agony while he was asking the Father to forgive them. They did not ask to be forgiven, but it was offered unconditionally, full and complete. But forgiveness is not a virtue and not a fruit of the Spirit. Therefore, unforgiveness and forgiveness are not in our souls but in our mind and body. They do not come naturally, even for a believer. They are a matter of the will for the mind to deal with using the power of the Holy Spirit.

What does Forgiveness Accomplish?
Moving past unforgiveness to forgiveness is the next step. Extending forgiveness removes guilt, ill feelings and remorse from both parties and may help to rebuild a relationship. Healthy relationships should be able to withstand the stress of misunderstandings. Forgiveness cannot be bought or sold. Forgiveness is not about fairness or justice but more about grace-giving. Forgiveness always needs to be gracefully extended and gracefully accepted.

The Unforgivable Betrayal?
One of the deepest hurts is an unfaithful spouse. Once the bond of trust has been broken, even after reconciliation, there is the dark cloud of skepticism. If it happened once, will it happen again? It takes a lot of time to work though unforgiveness to reach forgiveness. When Jesus had a woman caught in adultery brought to him, he freed her from guilt and told her to go and restore her relationship by being faithful. "Then neither do I condemn you," Jesus declared. "Go now and leave your life of sin" (John 8:11).

To sin is human, to forgive is divine. We are never closer to God's grace than when we admit our sin and cry out for pardon. We are never more like God than when we extend forgiveness fully and freely to those who have offended us.

When we get to heaven, Christ's forgiveness of us will be final and complete. "In him we have redemption through his blood, the forgiveness of sins, in accordance with the riches of God's grace" (Ephesians 1:7).

TOPIC #47
What is Biblically Good Mental Health?

Good mental health is being able to function each day with peace of mind. But what brings peace of mind? The six tenants of being at peace with yourself and others are:

1) **Having a strong identity.** You are a unique creation of God and he selected your DNA before you were born. No inferiority complexes permitted!
2) **Knowing that God and others love you.** Knowing that God's love is sufficient, even if others withhold love. Everyone needs to feel the warmth of being loved!
3) **Knowing that you are in a forgiven state by God and others.** No guilt trips needed!
4) **Knowing that what we do and think makes a difference, i.e. that your life has meaning and significance.** Have a purpose-driven life!
5) **Knowing that God is in control and that everything will ultimately work out for good.** No doubting required!
6) **Knowing that God allows suffering of all kinds** and even a death prognosis as a means to increase our faith, our intimacy with him and our love to and from others. No pity parties!

But knowing these things is only half of the truth. You need to feel them, too. Feelings may or may not be based on reality, but they certainly feel real. These emotions come out of nowhere but can be controlled with disciplined "reality thinking" (mental repetition of the facts). When we control our emotions with reality thinking, feelings do not control or overwhelm us. The alternative to this "what is" thinking is "what if," "if only," "could have," and "should have" thinking, which produces worry, anxiety, frustration or guilt. If this thinking continues over a period of time, it may cause depression.

Emotions are not sinful. Jesus, being fully human, had the full range of emotions. He experienced joy at the wedding in Canaan, anger when he drove out the moneychangers, compassion when he saw the crowds, depression at the garden of Gethsemane, sorrow when he cried at the death of Lazarus, betrayal at the hands of Judas and abandonment on the cross. Yet he was sinless.

Another aspect of good mental health is controlling memories. Memories can be recalled by concentrating our mental processes or can be spontaneous flashbacks. One of the results of trauma is that it leads memory to extremes of retention or forgetting. If they are intrusive or grotesque memories, they can lead to Post Traumatic Stress Disorder (PTSD). If we reminisce about good memories, they make us feel warm inside and joyful about life and can replace worry, depression and anger (Marriage & Family Journal, pgs. 449-453). Memories are the key to the future, not the past.

But what do we do when the glass is not half-full or half-empty, but empty--when tragedy strikes and there are no good alternatives. This is the time to access hope. Hope is the knowledge, conviction and expectation that God is in the business of converting bad into good. That is the reason why the darkest day in human history is called *Good Friday*.

TOPIC #48
The Book that Changes the World

Why has the Bible been banned in so many places? Why do people fear it? Why is the Bible the only book that over the years and until this day is criticized, ridiculed, discredited by atheists, agnostics and scoffers? They try to point out errors and inconsistencies. They try to discredit it by pulling things out of context. I doubt that most of them have read the entire Bible, yet they set themselves up as authorities on the subject.

Contrast that attitude with those of us who not only think of the Bible as *containing* the Word of God, but that it *is* the Word of God. We consider it Truth. Jesus said, "...the Truth will set you free" (John 8:32). We consider the Bible to be absolutely dependable. We use it daily for inspiration and to gain endless insights into how to manage our lives. It is a book that guides us and changes our lives.

Why do doubters feel so strongly opposed to the Bible? Maybe it is because the Bible teaches that men are free and to be under the control of God and only accountable to Him. It is a question of who is in charge. Men and governments have an innate propensity to want to be in control. The Scriptures teach that men should only put themselves under earthly powers voluntarily. Bible-believers believe that we should be accountable to society or the government or some other power, but only with our own consent.

Looking at history we can see how this book has changed the world.

In 1522 Martin Luther (1483-1546) opened the Scriptures to the common man by translating it into German, a readable language that most people could understand. Once the people could interpret the Scriptures, the power of the abuses of The Catholic Church was broken and the people were set free to worship God as their conscience led them. They saw that the required attendance at Mass was works, not grace, that Jesus was the mediator between God and man, not the Priest, that grace did not require penance, and that the selling of indulgences was a moneymaking scam. The Bible changed the course of human history.

William Tyndale (1494-1536) translated the Greek and Hebrew Bible into English. The King of England, Henry VIII, was angry with him because he knew the Bible would undermine his authority. Tyndale was imprisoned, beaten, exiled, and finally burned at the stake for his work. Anyone caught reading his version of the Bible was burned at the stake, and many were. But once people were able to read the Bible, they understood freedom. How could one book be such a big issue? Because it could change the world.

Our founding fathers were greatly influenced by the thinking of The Enlightenment (1648-1789) and referred to it in the Declaration of Independence as "Nature" and "Nature's God." Scholars were convinced that all of God's creation was rational so that it was possible for man to uncover laws that regulated society, politics, the economy, and even morality. The thought process of the Enlightenment was based on the Biblical account of creation where God made man in his own image. This meant that man could reason, imagine, and had a memory similar to God's. It also meant that he could fill his mind with knowledge, understanding, and wisdom. If men had freedom, they had unlimited potential. They knew that human beings were all created equal as a right. If man had the freedom to pursue his own best interests, everyone would benefit. This was based on Adam Smith's "invisible hand" idea of which the founders were well aware.

The Enlightenment also implied that God was a God of new things. God created new things like the universe and planet earth. He also reveals new things like man's discoveries – the wheel, magnetism, AC and DC electricity, AM and FM radio waves, air flight, the atom and nuclear fusion, silicon for computer chips, genetics and DNA, sending a man to the moon, and using unmanned space craft to explore the universe--to just name a few.

America's founders also knew that if we all start off with equal opportunity, some would better use their freedom causing unequal results. When you give life and liberty to people, the producing of wealth is natural. These unequal results drive the culture. This has produced the wealthiest and most culturally rich nation the world has ever experienced.

A man working in Mexico can earn $2.00 a day for his work. If he were in the United States he could earn $50 to $100 a day. Why the difference? Because we have economic, political, personal, and cultural freedom that promotes productivity that makes human capital more important than financial capital.

A country based on freedom requires people with Biblical virtues in order to have a just society. Consequently, Congress authorized the printing of Bibles for distribution to the public schools.

When there is revolution, the tyrants or religious leaders take over and people's freedom is lost. In the past and in the present, wherever the Bible goes, people gain economic, political and personal freedom. The Bible changes a culture, which benefits the people by reducing poverty, building families, and creating a more just society. It is this book that changes the world.

Following the end of World War II, Korea was divided into two counties, North and South. In 1950 North Korea invaded the

South, and by the end of fighting in 1953 both countries were in ashes.

Today North Korea is ruled by a tyrant who took total control. All personal, economic, and religious freedom has been lost. Bible-believers and those who are found hiding a Bible are arrested and sent to concentration camps. There are estimated to be 200,000 people in these camps where they are worked to death. Due to government control over agriculture, the country cannot even produce enough food to feed the people and there is starvation. Lack of electricity makes the whole country dark at night. Where there are not any Bibles, the people suffer.

South Korea, where there is religious and economic freedom, is thriving. Its economy is ranked 12th in the world (North Korea is ranked 125th), and there are 13 million Bible-believers who make up 30% of the population. Where the Bible is allowed, people flourish because it is this book that changes the world.

TOPIC # 49
Good and Evil

God is goodness and Truth. Satan is evil and the father of lies.
Evil is anything contrary to the nature or will of God. These two
forces are in conflict, in a struggle, a battle, a war.

These forces are in conflict in three different realms: in nature,
in the natural world, and in our hearts (soul).

An apple has two kinds of worms. When eggs are laid on the
tree's branches they produce worms that attack the apple from
the outside into the inside. When eggs are laid inside the apple
they produce worms that attack the apple from the inside out.
Because they are out of view it is more difficult to see how
much damage is being done. Just as there are two types of
worms there are two types of evil.

Evil from the Outside in--Nature
The good in nature came about at the time of creation when
God pronounced each step "good." When Adam and Eve
disobeyed God, God cursed the earth. Thus we have both good
and bad. The same plot of ground has both beautiful flowers
and noxious weeds. Some days are sunny and peaceful but the
next day may bring earthquakes, tornadoes, floods and drought.
These events are indiscriminate in that they affect some people
but not others. This randomness of peace and chaos seems
unfair. "He causes his sun to rise on the evil and on the good,
and sends rain on the righteous and the unrighteous" (Matthew
5:45). God does not always protect us from these things, but he
does give us the courage, hope, and ingenuity to deal with them.

Evil from the Outside in--The Natural World
The evil in the world affects us from the outside. Hitler in Nazi
Germany had his gas chambers, Stalin had his gulag, Mao had

his re-education program, Kim Il-sung had his work camps, and Saddam Hussein had his torture cells. Together they killed tens of millions of innocent people. Today we have murderers, rapists, kidnappers, drug addicts, drug dealers and Islamic terrorists who occupy our neighborhoods and invade our homes. We have 27 million people held in slavery. We have millions of people living in refugee camps under hopeless conditions. We have 2 billion people trapped in poverty, living on less than $2.00 per day. The world is an evil place that affects lots of innocent people.

God is a God of peace, but war was declared when Lucifer and his angels rebelled against God. The war is both celestial and earthly. Celestial war is described in Ephesians 6:12: "For our struggle is not against flesh and blood, but against the rulers, against the authorities, against the powers of this dark world and against spiritual forces of evil in the heavenly realms." Earthly wars can be just or unjust. Just wars can be used if they are to crush evil and establish good. God uses war to accomplish his will. Unjust wars are evil wars where an aggressive nation wants control over another nation

During World War II, General Eisenhower and General MacArthur ordered cities of the enemy bombed and invaded. They were honorable men and knew that thousands of innocent people would die. But they calculated by ending the war sooner they could save many more lives and go on to promote goodness. Thus the evil of war was used to serve God's purposes and to make peace.

These things are like worms that go from the outside to the inside.

Good from the Outside In
There is much good in this world. Every day billions of people produce goods and services for themselves and others. The

hungry are fed, the sick are healed, the homeless are given shelter, and people hear the good news of the gospel for the first time. People gather to have fun and be entertained. People care for each other. The world can be a good place.

Thus, the world is both a good place and bad place and there is conflict between them.

Evil from the Inside Out
God made man in his own image and everything went fine until Satan deceived Adam and Eve. Not only were their souls corrupted, every human being inherited a corrupt soul.

We have a worm inside of us.

While the dictators listed above had evil in their minds, they also had evil in their hearts. Each one of us has the potential for not controlling our minds and committing the same kind of evil acts. The human heart is desperately wicked, but because of the grace of God (Common Grace) we are still capable of good. When we invite Christ into our heart he gives us power over evil, but there is still a tension between good and evil. "I do not understand what I do. For what I want to do I do not do, but what I hate I do" (Romans 7:15).

Why do we need to understand good? Because we need to practice it every day in our personal lives, in our culture, and in our world. Why do we need to understand evil? Because we encounter it every day and we need to know how to deal with it. During World War II in North Africa there was an armored tank battle led by the American General George Patton against German Field Marshall Erwin Rommel. The Americans were winning when Patton declared, "I read your book." Because he had read Rommel's book he knew his tactics and was able to position the American tanks to outgun the Germans. Just as

Patton won the battle because he knew the tactics of the enemy, we must understand the tactics of The Great Deceiver.

While we can win the battles, we cannot win the war. Only when Christ returns and he casts the devil, his angels and his spirits into the abyss can we declare victory in the war with evil.

TOPIC # 50
Amazing Grace

One of our core values is *Grace*.

Grace is a unique virtue of the only true God whereby he chooses to treat us like we have never sinned. There is no need for God to count our shortcomings because there is nothing to count. But God's Truth has set the standard that makes us all consistently fall unacceptably short. God's justice requires we be accountable for the consequences we truly deserve. Ugh!

Grace defies reason and logic, but as best we can reason about God, Grace, Truth and Justice are inconsistent with each other until we apply the sacrifice of Jesus on the cross. If a person is a believer in Christ as Savior, every sin is covered and God can choose to see us as a fresh new creature. Christ's work reconciles Grace, Truth and Justice and in the process makes us new sin-free creatures. Yea!

Grace levels the playing field and makes our past moot. It frees us so it is safe to be open and honest. We can avoid the charades of "looking proper" and the pretense of "having it all together" because there is an abundant supply of grace. God's grace flowing to us, our grace flowing to others. We are new reconciled creatures in Christ.

Every day, approach God in prayer like a fresh new person, because you are!

Made in the USA
Charleston, SC
30 September 2014